22 STEPS TO A GREAT CATHOLIC PARISH

PRACTICAL AND **DOABLE** WAYS TO IMPROVE PARISH LIFE!

22 STEPS
TO A GREAT
CATHOLIC
PARISH

Practical and doable ways
to improve parish life!

JAMES N. REINHARDT

TWENTY
THIRD *23rd*
PUBLICATIONS
www.23rdpublications.com

TWENTY-THIRD PUBLICATIONS
A Division of Bayard
One Montauk Avenue, Suite 200
New London, CT 06320
(860) 437-3012 or (800) 321-0411
www.23rdpublications.com

Cover image ©iStockphoto/A-Digit

ISBN 978-1-58595-795-8
Library of Congress Catalog Card Number: 2010925836
Printed in the U.S.A.

Contents

Dedications, Acknowledgments, and Apologies

This book is dedicated first and foremost to Msgr. Michael D. Harriman, Pastor of St. Cecilia Church in San Francisco. His vision of church, the authenticity of his faith, and sense of celebration with which he lives his life make him the most effective priest and pastoral minister I have ever met. I treasure our friendship.

I am also forever in debt to the Youth Ministry staff of the San Francisco Archdiocese, the Northern California Youth Ministry Board, and the National Federation for Catholic Youth Ministry Board. As a member of these three groups in the 1980s, I learned more from them than I could ever remember. From a staff group of eight to a national board of nearly one hundred, I had the good fortune to be in the right place at the right time to see courageous, collaborative, giving, innovative ministry and to see the love of Jesus Christ pour out of people in ways that made a vision of church come alive.

I also thank the thousands of parish folks whom I have met over many years of consultations who showed me how to live Jesus' message every day.

Many thanks to those who have reviewed and critiqued drafts of this book, from its rough outline through nearly finished versions. Particular thanks to: Msgr. Michael Harriman; Beth Jordan, former Youth Ministry Director for the Diocese of Monterey, California; Peggy Ragsdale, former Youth Ministry Director for the Diocese of Oakland, California; Charles Ross of Petaluma, California, a colleague in youth ministry; Diane Elkins, Principal of the School of the Epiphany; and Sister Marilyn Miller, SNJM, Principal of St. Cecilia School, both of San Francisco. I also thank Sister Marilyn Murphy, SNJM, Pastoral Associate at the Church of the Epiphany in San Francisco, whose musings on the missed moment of grace following each Sunday Mass was the initial spark for this book.

Over the years, I have been intrigued by how much of the approaches of youth ministry have found their way into many broader areas of pastoral ministry. This book is a compilation and synthesis of all that I have discovered over the years. I thank God that I have been in the right place at the right time, surrounded by visionaries and innovators.

My theological and pastoral formation came in the main from two individuals. Theologically, Père Pierre Teilhard de Chardin, the great Jesuit paleontologist and theologian—a true twentieth-century Renaissance man—who died in 1955, has guided my life and my work. I discovered his writings just before moving into diocesan work in 1971, and the truth of his concepts has been my inspiration throughout my entire professional life.

Pastorally, I was touched early on by the work of Father Andrew Greeley, author, priest, and sociologist at both the University of Chicago and the University of Arizona. I had the good fortune to meet and hear him at St. Louis University in the late 1960s. While his fiction has never been to my taste, his views on the church (the big church and the parish), and our search for God as human beings have always resonated with me. (Now *there's* a California expression!)

Speaking of expressions, I want to offer one interesting aside: In researching every conceivable source for this book, I was struck by the curious phenomenon that many ministerial authors are still caught in traditional thinking. Just two examples: Many still speak of volunteers instead of ministers, and some still equate steward-ship with fundraising.

Lastly, need I remind anyone of the impact that the teachers of our youth had and still have on us? They can be like ghosts sit-ting on our shoulders, whispering admonitions into our ears. "Your principal is your pal." "Turkeys get done, people get finished." "A preposition is not a word to end a sentence with." You too can probably remember some of those clever reminders.

One of those reproaches had to do with never mixing person in a document. "If you start in the third person, stay in the third person!" As a storyteller, I have great difficulty following that rule in this book. (Or should I say that it has been very difficult for the author to follow that rule!)

The goal of each of this book's twenty-two chapters is to lay out a proposition around a particular area of church concern, to develop that problem or issue in broad conceptual terms and specific parish ones, and to become focused on the reader's parish with questions for their discussion that will begin big and then get specific. Laying out the issue and developing it is relatively easy to write in the ex-pository, third-person style.

At the same time, it is important to share personal experiences around an issue, to bear witness to the reality of it in my life. In that case, I use stories of my real-life events. This calls for writing in the first person, which seems more appropriate in these instances.

A series of questions for the reader to answer is usually found in the third part of each chapter, though sometimes they are contained in the main body of the text. Parish teams working for change will find that the answers lead to action steps. Here I have used the second person.

I have tried to be consistent throughout. However, if in a past life you were one of those strict grammarians who *never* mixed person. please forgive me.

James N. Reinhardt
San Francisco, California
May 2010

On Becoming a Great Parish

Picture this: a large circle of believers, a circle that faces both inward and outward, at once celebrating shared convictions and an invitation for others to join the circle. This is what we seek. How, though, do we put this image into more tangible terms? How do we make it real?

A friend once exclaimed, "It's hard to be a Christian by yourself!" It's true. Most of the message of Jesus comes down to how we relate to one another. The challenge is to live life together with others in the way he lived, in a revolutionary way. Doing so is just as difficult in today's pluralistic, materialistic, hypocritical world as it was in Roman-occupied Jerusalem when Jesus first gave us his message two thousand years ago.

My own world view has been deeply influenced by author and sociologist Fr. Andrew Greeley, equally well known for treatises on morality, commentary on the church in the modern world, and church-related novels. Some of his reflections on daily living that continue to guide me are these:

First, *love is at the core of the universe.* When forced to choose as to whether the world is bad or good, the Christian asserts that it is good

1

and that the manifestation of that goodness in Jesus is the ultimate proof that love is at the center of all things. "God Don't Make Junk," an expression, however grammatically butchered, that rose from East Coast teen retreats of the 1970s, was even made into buttons that the kids would wear. It served as a daily reminder of the goodness of God and the world. Perhaps each of us should wear that button as well.

> Every generous act of giving, with every perfect gift, is from above, coming down from the Father of lights, with whom there is no variation or shadow due to change. (James 1:17)

Second, *life triumphs over death, though only first by dying itself.* While a case can be made for a rational justification for the first proposition, that love is at the center of the universe, this second is more challenging because it can only be accepted by faith. No one alive can prove or disprove it.

> I call heaven and earth to witness against you today that I have set before you life and death, blessings and curses. Choose life so that you and your descendants may live. (Deuteronomy 30:19)

Third, Greeley contends, *the most appropriate form of human relationship is friendship,* both because it reflects the love that is at the core of the universe and because the act of trust that friendship demands reflects the triumph of life over death. There is an inherent truth in this third point, if one agrees to the first two. It has an acceptable "If-then" logic to it.

Fourth, *those who believe the truth of the first three propositions proclaim them to others essentially by celebrating.* We live in a world where we are taught that success comes by spending more money. The denial of that notion and the acceptance of a totally alternate way of looking at life, a way that so liberates us, can become a moment of staggering importance! It is an "Aha!" moment like no other! It is so powerful that celebrating is perhaps the only option.

Fifth, *that band of friends who celebrate love in the universe, the triumph of life over death, and friendship among all people, and by thus celebrating proclaim the Good News to others, is called the church.*

This is what the church is; this is what the church ought to be; this is what the church can be. If only...

What can we do to make our church like this? How do we find this or potentially create it in our daily lives? Perhaps for others, the monastic setting or communal life, or the world of sodalities or fraternal organizations or even the private "me and God" experience might be the place where God is found. The paradox of the modern age is that while many people apparently seek a relationship with God, fewer and fewer of them find it in traditional churches. In fact, the Pew study of 2008 paints a rather ominous picture for the future of mainstream religious denominations in America. (Chapter 4 covers these studies.) In spite of everything, the parish, more than any other source, remains the place to which more Catholics will turn. Since the parish is the place where most Catholics will have their encounter with Jesus and their experience with church, this book zeros in on that world.

Perhaps it would be more accurate to say that the parish is the place where Catholics *ought to be able* to have their encounter with Jesus and the way of life which He offers to us; the place where we can find others who share that desire and that experience; and the place where we can collectively celebrate this marvelous reality in our lives. Need it even be said that this is an elusive and rare find for most of us. Let us then look at steps that we can take to become more pro-active in seeking a deeper personal conversion and making our parish the place where that can happen for ourselves and for all those around us.

The center of parish life, the point where more parishioners come together than at any other moment, is, quite obviously, Sunday Mass, so this is where we begin. Each Roman Catholic Mass holds a unique moment, an extraordinary yet fleeting moment that often disappears, frequently unnoticed, as quickly as it appears.

We arrive for Mass. We seat ourselves, often at the end of the pew so as to escape quickly following dismissal. We settle in for sixty minutes (forty-five if we're lucky). We show visible annoyance when a latecomer dares to attempt to climb over our knees for a place in the middle of the pew. We hear two or three Scripture readings across an inadequate or poorly tuned speaker system. (Can you name even one reading from last Sunday?) We listen with varying degrees of interest to the homily. (What was Father's topic last week?) We frown at crying babies or fidgety children. We grunt rote responses to the Prayers of the People. (Do you remember even a single petition from last Sunday's Mass?) Then, we kneel and watch for the thousandth time or the five thousandth time as the priest consecrates and elevates the bread and wine. We recite together the prayer that we have known longer perhaps than any other in our lives, giving no thought whatsoever to the power of the words of Jesus. We shake the hand of our pew partner; or, during flu season, we keep our eyes on the altar and our hands folded to avoid human contact. We march forward, sometimes jostling for position, to receive Communion. We return to our seats, sit restlessly through pulpit announcements that seem not to end, and await the dismissal by a priest who sometimes can't stop preaching. Then, rushing to the parking lot, we drive away and lose the value of what has just happened.

A moment of grace has passed us by—unless we stop to reflect upon the import of these events. Move back in time a few minutes. As each of us heard the life-changing words of Scripture and consumed the consecrated bread, we brought Jesus Christ's presence into our minds and bodies and souls, into our lives. Individually and collectively, we were changed.

Rather than allowing this transformation to vanish before we leave the parking lot, imagine, if you will, the spiritual power we have in our grasp as we leave the church. What if we were to hold on to this communal moment of grace that just **renewed** us. Imagine how different the unfolding scenario would be if we allowed the transforming potential of the moment to take place. Imagine the collective power of the Christian assembly to change the world, starting with our departure from the parking lot and continuing throughout the day and week. *If only...*

Think about the countless encounters we have all week, with our spouse, our children, our neighbors, our work colleagues, the letter carrier, the grocery checkout clerk, our child's teacher, and all those whom we meet in all our week's transactions and adventures. Think about how all those encounters could be life-changing, if only we held to that transformation. An individual and communal moment of grace is there for us to grasp or ignore.

Sadly, Father's message went unheard or unheeded or unremembered. It might have been more difficult to remember that the small, quarter-shaped circle we placed upon our tongues was bread, much less Jesus' body. We responded to generic petitions that provided little if anything to stir our communication with God. The cacophonous choir did nothing to facilitate singing by the assembly. There was no Joyful Noise! Once again, we left the parking lot with no real moment of conversion in our reach.

In the ideal world, each of us would be conscious of and attentive to this moment. No nudging would be needed. We would be mindful of Sister's words from catechism class of long ago. We would willingly accept Father's stirring message. The power of Scripture would burn in our hearts. The presence of the Holy Eucharist would rouse us into individual and communal action. But, alas, few of us live in such an ideal world. Few of us belong to ideal parishes. (If you do, perhaps you should be authoring this book!)

In the following pages, practical, tangible, specific plans are offered for transforming your parish into a place where a truly Joyful
Noise can occur—not just good singing, but an inner and outer
conviction that this place is where I find God—where I find Him
(or Her) in the Sacraments, in the person of the priest, in those
others who join me here, and in myself.

What happens in your assembly? Is there a Joyful Noise? Let us
then look for ways to find such an experience in our parish. We
know that this is possible. We have seen other churches where the
joy and excitement of belonging are so palpable that the members nearly squeal with delight, places where it's easy to be good,
where the fellowship and bonds are so strong that we long for such
a feeling in our own church. A heart-to-heart talk with the leaders of such churches would certainly reveal that this result did not
occur easily or quickly. These churches are great because they collectively determined and embraced certain values, they set about
consciously to make their church great, they worked at it for a long
time, they never stopped, they were always open to change, and,
above all, they **never** took their members for granted. It is possible for you to get there, too. You and others of like mind can
make your parish great, perhaps greater than it already is. The steps
contained in this book can help you get there. This goes beyond
(or perhaps deeper than) programs, though. What is needed is a
change of thinking about the way we are church. Thus, if a particular chapter here seems to be close to meeting your needs but not
quite on target, change it. These topics offer starting points, not
finish lines.

Browse through the twenty-two topics. First glance through the
basics of those that interest you, and then read in detail the steps

that seem most relevant to your needs. Very likely, you will find that your parish already works well in ways such as that described in some categories. Wonderful! Use those chapters as checks or benchmarks to compare your experience with that suggested by the author.

Move to others where you find you are in most need. Make a list. Then the questions arise. Do we begin to attempt the things most easily accomplished? Or do we seek to solve those problems in most need of solution? How many steps can we try to accomplish simultaneously? Are these chapters organized in any sequential order? Where does the pastor fit into these plans?

The last question needs to be answered first. Simply put, no authentic, longstanding change can be made in a parish without the full support and ownership of your pastor. The pastor ought to be the initiator and the animator of such change. But then, no such change can be made without such ownership by the whole parish! No one needs flash-in-the-pan gimmicks. We are thus faced with two major tasks. The pastor must be at the very center of this movement, and the people of the parish need to be right there by his side—from the very beginning.

One person cannot expect to own a sole copy of this book, keep it to him(her)self, and individually try to make such changes happen. At the risk of sounding like a commercial to sell lots of copies, steps toward change might be something like these:

1. Begin with an acknowledgment that you are seeking change. After all, the very title of this book implies that you want to get from where you are to a better place. Begin knowing that the process will be long, stressful, winding, filled with surprises, difficult at times, easy at others, painful at times, joyful at others, frustrating at times, exhilarating at others. It will be filled with moments of emptiness and moments of celebration. Change is like that.

2. Thinking outside the box is the operative expression. These times are different from our growing-up years. The problems we face are new ones. Old methods and old solutions probably won't work any longer. We need to look for new solutions to today's problems. One constant remains, however. All the while, the Holy Spirit will be at your side.

3. If you are not the pastor, now is the time to immediately engage him in this process. No further steps should be taken until he is fully involved and committed. If your parish is temporarily without a pastor, you should probably do a realistic assessment of how much change can be accomplished until leadership is determined. If you are permanently without a pastor and are, in fact, a mission parish, take your concerns to the leadership of your parent parish. In many cases, that pastor may be happy to see pastorally based leadership emerge from the mission parish.

4. Engage all who are interested in seeing a great parish to informal discussions about their levels of satisfaction and what might be on their wish lists. Invite everyone to join in the sharing. Casual opportunities like coffee and doughnuts after Sunday Masses are great for this. You might start there to quickly learn who is interested. Look for other parishioners whose zeal for commitment to their faith and the church is readily apparent, like veterans of Marriage Encounter, Cursillo, or the Charismatic Renewal. If your parish already has Small Christian Communities, ask those members. Ask to be invited to meetings of different parish organizations to get their thoughts. Listen to the chatter on the steps of the church after Mass. Do everything possible to spread the word: bulletin messages, pulpit announcements, vestibule posters, flyers, e-mails—everything!

5. Circulate copies of this book among those who seek such change and want to work for it. It is written as an easy read, with lots of stories and thought-provoking questions, designed to stir the imaginations and stimulate movement for parish renewal.

6. Constantly keep the door open to others who learn of such discussions and want to join in on them. Invite everyone who has an interest or an opinion. Don't discriminate. Don't exclude those who disagree with your thoughts. In fact, you would do well to intentionally invite others with whom you know you will disagree so as to get the broadest possible range of ideas! Remember: **Wisdom resides in the group and in the Holy Spirit,** and not just in a select few.

7. Provide many different entry opportunities for others to join in. *Never* close the door to others. It's never too late to get on the bandwagon for change! One pastor once said, "I'll love them into change."

8. Remember to pray, pray, pray. Not just a routine "Our Father" at the beginning of a meeting, but genuine shared prayer. Yes, it takes time. Read Chapter 2 for a further discussion of this topic.

9. *Always* report to the larger parish about such sharing. Do this regularly and constantly—at every step of the process. Don't keep this a secret. Never allow a perception of exclusivity to emerge. Always presume that your parish is composed of people of good will. The broadest possible ownership of this process, from the first stages, will go a long way to assure success.

10. Set reachable goals that will result in successes, especially in the early stages. Don't set yourself up for frustrating failure.

11. Look at steps that call upon personal growth or change or evangelization before taking other larger, system-wide steps.

12. Then, look at the changes you plan. Decide which are built upon earlier ones. Look at which ones need to be done in sequence, those that rely upon an earlier step for success.

13. *Nothing* in this book is etched in stone. Everything is subject to modification to meet your particular needs. Moreover, no one can say with any certainty that there are exactly twenty-two steps toward change. Your parish might need three or five or ten or thirty-seven! If one constant exists from the author's forty years of parish consultations, it is that every parish is different!

14. Remember: a Joyful Noise isn't always harmonious or easy on the ears, especially at the beginning. A certain amount of chaos is good for the soul!

15. You're talking about big-time, *systemic change* here, about how Catholics live their faith, about how they see their parish, not about superficial fluff. Change and growth are part of the natural order of the universe, but not everyone in your parish will accept that. Keep these realizations in front of you always.

16. Remember, too, that change—true, genuine, longstanding change—is a function of many different factors: shared vision, openness to the views of everyone, effective leadership in facilitating change, sensitivity to the impact of accumulated change on those asked to implement it, and, perhaps most important, broad ownership by everyone involved through consensual agreement. *Everyone*—not just the leadership.

17. Change is stressful. Change in the church is especially so, because it is related to the comfort level of the assembly. Remember: for some, God alone dictated the way everything has been done since time immemorial and change is sacrilegious. In some parishes it is not God alone. It is the late pastor who guided the parish in one fixed direction for decades, who could make no mistakes, who was, thus, like God, sitting perhaps at His right hand, and whose ghost still hovers over the parish, having entrusted a few loyal followers to monitor that no new pastor does anything that he would not have approved of. If you are old enough to remember when the priest began to say Mass in English at an altar that faced the people, you will know exactly how difficult change can be!

18. **Remember: The word "you" is the same in English, whether in singular or plural usage. Look back over these steps and make certain that the images in your mind are those of the plural "you" and not you alone.**

19. Swallow hard, breathe deeply, and begin!

Who Should Use This Book—and Why
Who Ought to Be Reading This?

A s the author, I can see the people in the parish for whom I have written this book. Who are you? In my mind's eye, I see a person browsing the book display at a ministry conference—someone who picks up this book and spots its potential value to the parish. Lay, religious, or ordained—it makes no difference. I see a pastor beginning to identify key parish leaders who can work through the issues and challenges presented in this book. I see a pastoral associate or a parishioner taking a copy to the pastor, suggesting its use with the pastoral council.

In my mind's eye, I envision a small group of dedicated Catholics using this book, gathered perhaps in a rectory dining room, a parish office, a classroom, someone's living room, a neighborhood coffee shop, or in any one of many other meeting spaces everywhere. They are meeting in parishes of all kinds—large, small, rich, poor, urban, rural. Their accents may be different. They may dress differently. They may or may not have a sizable parish staff. Their parish plants may vary from a sprawling suburban park-like campus to

tiny buildings stretched far beyond their limits for meeting and activity space. Their points of view may be different. Many of them,
however, may come to discover that they share a general notion
that their parish could be better, that it needs to grow and change.
They may come from all over the political spectrum. They may have
many different views about the role of the parish. But their catho-
licity is their commonality.

What you have in common is a strong desire for change in
your parish—balanced, planned change, strategic change, durable
change that moves step by step to a better place, closer to becoming
a great parish, an excellent parish.

■ Where Do We Begin?

"Is there any order to these chapters?" you ask. The answer is "Yes—
sort of."

Sunday Liturgy (Chapter ①) is first because it is the most important thing that your parish does, but liturgical change will be authentic only when it reflects a comparable change in parish thinking. Arguably, if the Eucharist celebrates all that we are as church,
it ought to be covered last, so as to include all the changes and re-
thinking that occurs during your movement to greatness. It is first
here, however, because so many of the parts of the Sunday time together that parishioners see and feel can easily be improved, bringing about an immediate change for the better. Other more subtle
changes, like openness to prayer, the level of satisfaction with
parish membership, and joy around spending time together, will
take longer to accomplish and might not be immediately apparent.
In the final analysis, Eucharist is first, last, and always.

Prayer (Chapter ②) is right there with Liturgy because everything
in parish life (and personal life) must be rooted in prayer.

Practical definitions of the faith development process—evangelization, catechesis and ministry—and the place of relational min-

istry at the heart of it (Chapter 3) are there, too, because they are central to what the parish ought to be about and how people feel about belonging to it. For many, this will be a refreshing change from the depersonalization they have experienced in the past in their parishes.

Along with faith development come steps in encouraging greater shared ownership of parish life (Chapter 4) and a total revamping of the definition of stewardship (Chapters 5 and 6)—very foundational issues.

The chapters in the middle of the book take on many different specific topics important to all parishes—inviting others to share in its ministries (Chapter 7), recognizing and acknowledging everyone's gifts (Chapter 8), the importance of first impressions (Chapter 9), honoring your parish history (Chapter 10), Catholic school issues (Chapter 11 and 12), saving the earth (Chapter 13), and communication issues (Chapters 14 through 16).

Chapters 17 and 18 cover structural issues of balance in the life of your parish, both as one large group and as a cluster of small groups. Chapter 19 analyzes the single biggest demographic gap for most parishes—youth and young adults.

Consensus-seeking and Planning (Chapters 20 and 21) are placed near the end for perhaps obvious reasons. Use them to better assess steps in your movement toward becoming a great parish.

The Four Marks of the Church (Chapter 22) are very definitely considered last because I believe that they should function as the most fundamental report card for the "right"-ness of what we are about as church. After all, they have served that purpose for nineteen hundred years!

■ A Few Remaining Points

- **When you see text that looks like this,** I suggest that this is a foundational or extremely important point.

- I have intentionally placed all bibliographic and other references at the end of each chapter to make them easier to find and use, especially since so many Web sites are discussed.

Now, jump right in with both feet!

CHAPTER 1

Meeting Your Sunday Obligation
and Other Thoughts on Celebrating the Eucharist

> The gaze of the Church is constantly turned to her Lord,
> present in the Sacrament of the Altar, in which she dis-
> covers the full manifestation of his boundless love.
>
> *Ecclesia De Eucharistia*, Sec. 1, Pope John Paul II

First, last, and always: Liturgy is the single most important event in
the life of the parish. It is the time of the week when more parishioners come together than any other moment. Put aside parish organization meetings, working project committees, and Small Christian
Communities. All these smaller gatherings are important—they help
make the parish function—but it is only the weekend eucharistic
celebrations that bring the entire people of God together.

It stands to reason, then, that more effort should go into improving and maintaining the quality of the liturgical experience
than any other single program or event in parish life. **Your weekend
liturgical celebrations should be a microcosm of all that the parish is
trying to become.** Look at every aspect of these celebrations to make
them the moments that parishioners look forward to each week.

Jesus did not simply appear in a group, pray with them, and disappear from them. He spent time with them. He lived with them. We should do the same at our weekend liturgies. Mass schedules need to be spaced in such a way that there is time for gathering before the Mass and socializing afterward. Something as simple as doughnuts and coffee after Mass gives everyone an opportunity to check in with one another.

Remember: Not everyone can make the parish the center of their lives. Young couples with children in school, holding down perhaps more than one job, juggling homework, Little League, ballet lessons, and other more mundane tasks like cutting the grass and cleaning the garage, may find that Sunday morning is their only opportunity to be present for any parish activity. This is all the more reason that this time needs to be given the highest possible place in parish life.

Stand at the back of your church during the largest Mass of the weekend. One pastor I know does this regularly. Put yourself in the shoes of the person in the pew—especially the back pew. Later, go on a walk through your plant and consider these issues.

■ The Environment or Atmosphere

Appearance

Put on fresh eyes. Is the plaza in front of the church well kept? Is it free of litter? Are shrubs well groomed? Grass cut? The garden well tended? If you were a newcomer, would you be able to look around and determine where the parish office is?

What is your first impression upon entering the church? What does the condition of the vestibule tell you about the people's pride in their parish? Is it clean and orderly? Can the parish mission statement be seen anywhere in the vestibule? Can you find appropriate information on the bulletin boards? What about a copy of this week's bulletin or flyers for other programs? Is there a sense of welcome? Does the vestibule tell you that the people of the parish are glad that you came? Are the restrooms unlocked? Are they clean? Are paper supplies and hand soap stocked?

2. In the Church

Are the aisles clean and free of litter? As you walk through the aisles, are missalettes and songbooks properly stored in pew racks? Are the pews free of clutter? Have crumpled, left-over Sunday bulletins been removed?

Look up to the sanctuary. Even in the darkness when the church is empty, is the sanctuary clean? Have wilted flowers been removed? Is the sanctuary lit with candles, signifying the presence of the Holy Eucharist in the tabernacle? Is the building lit well enough for you to feel safe?

3. Lighting

Ask your Liturgy Committee to visit the church at night. Turn on all the lights, just as they are at Mass. Are all light bulbs operating? Have any directional spotlights gotten nudged off kilter as bulbs were changed over the years, resulting in dark zones in the sanctuary? Are the pulpit and cantor locations well lit? What about the light illuminating the congregation, especially around the edges? Sit down and try to read a missalette in different congregational areas.

4. Sound (NEEDS ATTENTION)

Remember: The projection of sound will be different when the church is empty and when it is full. Testing the microphones and speakers at 2:00 in the afternoon will produce a very different experience from that of a slightly hard-of-hearing parishioner sitting three rows from the rear of the church at a packed children's Mass. In one parish, the deadest sound zone was the front pew, since the loudspeakers high above it were aimed at the larger church and missed the people sitting in that pew altogether. Do the microphones and speakers produce a crisp, clear sound that everyone can hear and understand from anywhere in the building? Do the microphones used by the choir and instrumental musicians (like the guitarist) produce the desired results? Ask some of your older parishioners.

Some parishes have recognized the increasing number of members with hearing impairments and have installed a particular assistive product called a "loop system." Just as a coffee shop might install a "wi-fi" system for wireless computer customers, churches can install the loop system hardware, and hearing-impaired members can use a loop listener to pick up the sound more clearly. For more information, just do a Google search on "loop systems for the deaf."

B. ■ The Ministers

The Priest Celebrant

Priest celebrants should welcome visitors at the beginning of each Mass. One pastor asks any visitors to stand to receive the applause of the assembly. At the end of the Mass, he thanks everyone for being part of the community celebration.

Priests must approach each Mass as a fresh, new experience—a tall order. If the Eucharistic Prayer or Lord's Prayer is read too quickly, or with little or no personal conviction, the person in the pew will have the same experience. Learn to slow down and proclaim instead of reading. One priest talked of making his lenten resolution to re-train himself to make the words of the Mass meaningfully presented. He chose to use a sung Eucharistic Prayer, which by its very nature brought the tempo and cadence down to where each word could be understood. We know that the words of the eucharistic celebration are meaningful, but do we proclaim them that way and do we hear them that way?

Priests must deliver homilies that share how human they are and not how much they know. Save the theological lecture for a Monday night series. Help me to live my life more like Jesus did. Tell me stories that connect Scripture to the reality of my life. Share with me the truth about life to be found in the Scripture readings for this week. After all, the readings are sometimes so rooted in first-century life and experience that we may miss their meaning. Let me know what struggles that you as a priest and, more importantly, as a man face that I can relate to. What does this Gospel tell me that will help me deal with my kids this afternoon? Or on Monday at work? Or to improve my relationship with my spouse? Or to find meaning in the latest cataclysm around the world? Parishioners will remember those messages more than any complex dissertation on the meaning of the Trinity. We live in the era of the twenty-four-hour news cycle. We can either become numbed to the constant barrage or we can be helped to find meaning in the events through our faith.

Consider asking the parish Liturgy Committee to take on the regular evaluation of all weekend homilies. After all, the quality of the homily is arguably the single greatest variable at most weekend Masses. This is, admittedly, a challenging idea. The purist might argue that participation in the Eucharist has its own intrinsic value, regardless of how well it is executed from a human point of view. After all, the miracle of Jesus' presence in the Eucharist cannot be argued and has nothing to do with how well the celebrant presents a homily. Nonetheless, the church on any given Sunday is full of human beings, each of whom is at his or her own stage of faith development, each of whom brings a unique state of readiness for the message presented. We owe it to everyone present to help them have the best possible experience.

Lay Liturgical Ministries

Ministry Training

Does the Liturgy Committee provide ongoing, regular, and separate training for all lay liturgical ministers? (Don't make ushers attend a session that includes training for lectors as well.) Every liturgical minister, no matter how experienced, needs to be encouraged and cajoled into attending training. Just because someone has been an usher at the 9:30 Mass for thirty-five years doesn't mean he understands that his ministry is one of hospitality and not traffic control, or even that his work is a ministry and not a task.

Proclaiming Scripture

Most lectors do not come to this ministry with public speaking experience. Training for lectors should include lots of time at the pulpit, with the microphones on. Projection and enunciation are critical. Lectors should always rehearse their readings, including practicing the readings out loud ahead of time. Discuss the difference between reading and proclaiming. Fellow off-duty lectors should listen during Masses so that they can give feedback to one another.

Music Leadership

Is it the duty of the organist and cantor to facilitate singing or to dazzle the congregation with a virtuoso performance? Make sure that everyone has the same answer to this question. Is there a reasonable mix of familiar music and new songs so as not to overwhelm the assembly? Does the music leader "warm up" the assembly with rehearsal of new songs or responses before Mass? Does he or she constantly affirm them for their participation? Are song numbers prominently posted throughout the church in such a way that they can be seen from anywhere in the building?

Pulpit Announcements

Are parishioners reminded to turn off cell phones before Mass? Even the best-intentioned person can forget to do so. The reminder should be friendly, and this is one subject well suited to a bit of humor.

Even though there might be a lot of pressure from interested groups, try to minimize the number of pulpit announcements that merely repeat what can be read in the bulletin. Remember: If announcements are made near the end of the Mass before the final dismissal, most people want to get home for the beginning of the early NFL game. Strategically plan appropriate pulpit announcements.

Ministers of Hospitality *(WELCOMING)*

The importance of hospitality cannot be overstated. Regular parishioners need to feel they are not being taken for granted. Newcomers need to feel they are being noticed. Being approached by someone with a smile and an outstretched hand might be a very new experience for some. It can only help; it can't hurt. One pastor said that he asked everyone in his hospitality ministry training to say to themselves before each Mass, "Company's coming! We need to get everything ready for company!"

Greeters

Provide ministry badges for greeters. Greeters should be present at each entrance to the church, not just the main doors. This is a ministry of hospitality.

Newcomers and visitors especially should feel that someone representing the parish is welcoming them.

- The first issue is to ask greeters to keep their eyes open for visitors. That can be challenging in a large congregation.

- Greet them warmly at the door. Introduce yourself to them, engage them in conversation, and invite them in. Connect them to an usher who will escort them to an open pew.

- If they are new to the area, try to answer any questions they might have.

- At the end of Mass, walk them back out of the church and *invite them back!*

- Ushers can and should be doing the same thing for people inside the church.

Ushers

Provide ministry badges for ushers. Ushers have important duties both before and during the Mass. If ushers arrive early, they can walk the aisles and pick up crumpled bulletins from earlier Masses and help to make the church look ready for visitors. Help them understand that theirs, too, is a ministry of hospitality more than crowd control. Encourage them to smile when ushering people to their pew. Invite women to share in this ministry. Their warmth and sense of greeting may be a refreshing change in some parishes. Most latecomers are timid about trying to climb over someone sitting at the end of a pew to find an available seat. Ushers should become pro-actively aware of available seats so that no one is left standing in the aisle. Ushers should refrain from any whispered conversations. One person's whisper is another's annoying interruption.

Ushers should be sensitive to those with physical impairments and offer special assistance to them. Ushers should watch for infirm persons, perhaps using crutches or a walker, who have difficulty finding a place to sit. Locate a place and escort the individual forward. Since most infirm persons seem to want to stay independent, offer an arm for assistance only gently or when asked.

When taking up the collection, smile and offer eye contact with donors. Doing so shows appreciation for their gifts. Whisper a "thank you" to small children placing envelopes in the basket. Be patient with those searching their purses or pockets for their envelopes. There is time.

Ushers should also be able to experience personal value from participating in the Eucharist and should never be so busy with money-handling duties that they miss key moments of the Mass, such as the Eucharistic Prayer. Ushers should have the last pew reserved for them so that they may be able to put ushering duties aside and participate as fully as possible. Having such a reserved place avoids the need to climb over others when it is time to take up the collection or facilitate people movement for Communion.

Most large church buildings, especially those with long rectangular styles modeled on the Roman basilica, seem to have a life of their own at the rear of the church that has nothing whatever to do with what is going on at the altar. Ushers should do everything possible to get standees seated, limit the sound of slamming doors made by late arrivals and early departers, work with those who receive cell phone calls and feel compelled to answer them, herd small children who have escaped from their parents' pews, and encourage errant teenagers who simply want to pick up a bulletin and determine which priest is the celebrant so they can prove to their parents that they were there. No small job, the work of an usher.

SHOW APPRECIATION

■ Sermons I Wish That I Had Heard
Sometimes it's fun just to get things off your chest!

To Those Who Bring Cell Phones to Church If you're going to leave your phone turned on, at least pick a religious tune for your ring tone so we can all sing along. And if you feel compelled to answer a call, please wait until you're outside before beginning your conversation.

Instructions to Ushers Please leave the police whistles at home and put a smile on your face instead. Remember to keep an eye on those who just lean against the back wall in case they fall asleep and start to tip over. Jostle any snorers you hear. When you're taking up the collection, have change available for anyone who needs to break a dollar bill.

To Those Who Arrive After the Homily and Leave Before Communion Why bother getting up so early? Just stop by on a Wednesday afternoon for a brief visit. Make it easy on yourself.

To Those Who Claim the Good Seat at the Ends of Open Pews Please don't stick out your foot and try to trip anyone who dares cross over your knees. The parish is not responsible for broken bones.

To Those Who Still Put Coins in the Collection Basket The jingling of coins is keeping some Mass-goers awake. Please use quiet money instead.

There, now. Doesn't that make you feel much better!

THE BIG QUESTIONS

As was stated at the beginning of this chapter, the weekend liturgical celebration should be a microcosm of all that the parish is trying to become. Should change in the way you do liturgy then be the first thing or the last thing you do? Both. In fact, liturgical improvement should be first, last, and always!

A starting point will be to follow the lead suggested in this chapter. Take a walk through the church. This chapter can serve as a checklist. Carry this book with you and answer the questions as you move from area to area. Your agenda for change will quickly become clear to you.

BIBLIOGRAPHY AND ASSOCIATED RESOURCES

The entire text of *Ecclesia De Eucharistia*, an encyclical letter issued by Pope John Paul II on Holy Thursday, April 17, 2003, may be found at the Vatican's Web site, www.vatican.va. The document may be purchased in book form from the U.S. Bishops' Conference at their Web site, www.usccb.org, or at (800) 235-8722.

You might want to look at www.buildingchurchleaders.com. While slightly evangelical in tone, they offer lots of good resources—mostly downloadable, some free, others low-priced—that can easily be translated into Catholic usage. Look at their title "Usher/Greeter—Tips and Training for a Critical Ministry" (Store Code OG07) as an example of th

CHAPTER 2

Put Prayer at the Center of Everything

Beloved Jesus, anoint us to do your will. May the joy of your dwelling in us draw us closer to each other. Expand our vision to recognize your plan; warm our hearts by the flame of your love; open our lips so that we can speak your Word; extend our arms so that we can embrace each other as your people; speak to us so that we can discern the role you have for us, your Body, your Church. Fill us with your Holy Spirit, empowering us to become vital expressions of growth in your changing church. Your Kingdom is now! Help us discover and live your will. Amen.

"Prayer in Time of Change,"
written by the Office of Pastoral Planning,
Roman Catholic Diocese of Albany, New York

There was a time when most parishes were full of priests and sisters. For the regular person in the pew, these were the "holy people" who did the praying for all of us. They were perceived, rightly or wrongly, as spending their lives in candle-lit chapels, with rosaries or breviaries in hand, communicating with God for all of

26

us. Many seemed to be separated from the world, living in a distinct reality where they communicated with God and the saints in ways that we laypeople could never do. They didn't go to movies. Sisters didn't drive cars. They lived only for their work in their parishes and schools. These men and women brought a spiritual presence into the parish that benefited every member—although we seldom thought of them as men and women. For better or worse, this made Catholic churches unique among Christians, and we took comfort in that.

Now, parishes are very different. Most parishes and schools are staffed by laypeople, who live in the secular world and did not have that same intensive spiritual formation that sister-teachers once did. Consequently, parishes must pro-actively develop plans for spiritual formation and prayer among members that might have been done by the religious in earlier times. Older Catholics are used to rote responses and memorized prayers. Spontaneous, verbal shared prayer was until recently unknown to most, except perhaps members of the Charismatic Renewal or veterans of Cursillo, Marriage Encounter, or similar movements. Without a deep prayer life, however, the parish is little more than a social club.

Ministry leaders must learn to put prayer at the center of every activity. It is a prayerful life that will make your parish a great one. Programs and smiles and cleanliness are important, but a deep and authentic parish prayer life is the most significant, because it immediately tells the parishioner or visitor what is essential.

Begin with the readings for each Sunday. Make them an integral part of the prayer life of the parish, as they are for the universal church. Each Sunday, at every Catholic church throughout the entire world, all parishioners share the same Scriptures. The church is one at that moment, as every Catholic hears one of the many great stories of our tradition. Now, go one step further.

Consider using the readings for the coming Sunday for shared prayer and reflection at all meetings and activities each week.

People at all meetings and gatherings—of the staff, the pastoral council, committees and commissions, groups and organizations— can listen to, reflect upon, pray about and share personal thoughts about one or more of the upcoming Sunday's readings. As with all areas of ministerial change, the leadership should model the new behavior they expect from everyone. Change of prayer style should begin with the staff and the pastoral council. As these two groups become comfortable with this approach, it will filter more easily throughout all areas of parish life. **The goal here is that the active parishioner will have heard and reflected upon the readings, perhaps more than once, well before coming to Mass on any given Sunday.**

Look to print resources, such as *Exploring the Sunday Readings*, published by Twenty-Third Publications. It covers the readings for a month of Sundays in each issue. It offers a significant narrative reflection on each of the Sunday readings, followed by several questions to guide either personal reflection or group sharing. Go to www.23rdpublications.com for more information. *Sunday By Sunday*, published by Good Ground Press, the publishing arm of the St. Paul Province of the Sisters of St. Joseph of Carondelet, works in much the same fashion. Check out www.goodgroundpress.com for information. There are many others like these that provide similar resources. www.pastoralplanning.com offers a "Question of the Week" for each Sunday of the year, which invites people to listen to the Sunday Scriptures and prayerfully discuss their meaning. Each publisher offers a slightly different approach, but the goal is the same: to create and sustain a sense of community within the group. One or another style of faith sharing will surely match the needs of your group.

These sources offer the kind of resource needed to help with this process. They provide the pastoral insights needed for the kind of rich prayer sharing that will take place even when groups meet without clergy leadership. Ask the pastor to subscribe to such a series with enough copies so that each group or ministry receives one each week. Curiously, if you strip away all the specifics, these questions always seem to boil down to just a few: How is God speaking to you right now? How is God touching your life?

Model this approach to prayer at all parish gatherings as needed. Provide ongoing formation for all ministry leaders so that they are comfortable leading prayer. In time, more and more parishioners will become at ease with it.

Unfortunately, many parish groups can become so task-oriented that they fail to see their meetings as opportunities for ministry. Often, individuals have been selected for organizational leadership more for their commitment to the task than for their prayer life. A quick "Our Father," "Hail Mary" and "Glory Be" might be the only prayer at a meeting. After all, there's lots of work to get done. As a result, this emphasis on prayer might be new territory for many parishioners.

Offer an all-day exposition of the Blessed Sacrament once each month, perhaps on First Fridays. Do this in a special place, like a side chapel, where visitors can go on these days for a few moments of quiet time with God.

Some parishes keep a Chapel of the Blessed Sacrament open twenty-four hours a day. Admittedly, a church building open all night can present security challenges that must be addressed. First and foremost, parishioners must find the church a safe place to enter, at whatever hour. A decision to offer this service will require serious thought and planning. Parishioners sign up for thirty- or sixty-minute blocks for meditation and prayer. Some will do it at 6 AM on their way to work, or on the way to pick up the kids after school, or right before a parish meeting in the evening, or at midnight on Wednesdays. Those who faithfully do this find that it becomes an important part of their lives.

Offer evangelization retreats for adults regularly. (Evangelization and its partner concept, catechesis, are covered in the next chapter.) Offer them at different times so one or another will fit each person's schedule: perhaps Sunday afternoon, perhaps three evenings in a row, perhaps Saturday morning. Listen to people's needs and the timing will become apparent. These retreats can be built around faith sharing and peer-to-peer ministry—parishioner to parishioner.

Make Small Christian Communities available for ongoing support. (For more details, see Chapter 18 where this approach is covered.) They provide a sense of belonging and assistance with a prayer-based spirituality.

Follow up constantly to see that it happens and that they don't simply fall back on the Lord's Prayer. Continue to provide resources and prayer models for group leaders.

Ministry leaders must face the reality that most adult Catholics stopped learning about their faith when they graduated from Catholic school or were confirmed when they were thirteen years old. If we want our adult Catholics to have genuine adult faith lives, we must help them move from an early adolescent experience to one consistent with their stage in life.

That having been said, don't mix up teaching about prayer with praying. While it is possible to teach people that there are four kinds of prayer (praise, petition, confession, thanksgiving), it is not possible to teach anyone how to pray. We don't learn to pray by listening to a lecture on prayer. We learn to pray by listening to and then by sharing in prayer led by others. Gradually, we become more comfortable doing it because in prayer we open our hearts to God's presence in us. God was always there, but becoming persons of prayer allows us to acknowledge God more freely.

That's why you should never say, "Let us put ourselves in the presence of God," when convening a group in prayer. After all, God is there already. It's better to say, "Let us remember that we are in the holy presence of God."

THE BIG QUESTIONS

Catholics don't have the long tradition of spontaneous, shared prayer that Pentecostals do. Catholics are used to memorized prayers recited in groups. What is needed to make prayer an experience of the heart? This change in personal spirituality is essentially the same as that called for in the broader discussions on faith development later in this book. Spiritual growth will help parishioners move toward a more personal prayer experience. You can have confidence knowing that spiritual growth and prayer growth will happen concurrently. Steps can be taken sooner, though, to encourage more shared prayer, like those described earlier that use the Sunday readings. How can you begin this process in your parish? Identify all the councils, commissions, committees, and organizations of the parish. Who is the key person in each group who can help move them toward a richer prayer experience in their meetings? What help and support must you first give to those individuals to enable them in this change?

BIBLIOGRAPHY AND ASSOCIATED RESOURCES

"Prayer in Time of Change" was written by the Office of Pastoral Planning of the Roman Catholic Diocese of Albany, New York.. Go to their Web site (www.rcda.org) for information about their pastoral planning process.

The three Web sites described in the text—www.23rdpublications.com, www.goodgroundpress.com, and www.pastoralplanning.com—are particularly helpful in assisting parish groups with prayer built around the Scripture readings of the following Sunday. *Catechist* magazine (www.catechist.com) also offers "Lessons for the Sunday Gospels" on all the Sundays of each month.

CHAPTER 3

Evangelization, Catechesis
and Other Jargon Words

> Let us strengthen our commitment and intensify our efforts to help the adults in our communities be touched and transformed by the life-giving message of Jesus, to explore its meaning, experience its power, and live in its light as faithful adult disciples today. Let us do our part with creativity and vigor, our hearts aflame with love to empower adults to know and live the message of Jesus. This is the Lord's work. In the power of the Spirit it will not fail but will bear lasting fruit for the life of the world.
>
> *Our Hearts Were Burning Within Us*, #183, U.S. bishops

In Diocesan Youth Ministry, we spoke of the horde of baptized but unevangelized youth. So many young Catholics had no idea of *why* they were Catholic, they just *were*. We did, and still do, lose many of them to aggressive fundamentalist groups, where their young members know exactly why they are there. The larger Catholic Church shares this curious dichotomy. Those of us who were born into the church may not always know why we are here. We are Catholic because we have always been Catholic. In a world where religious values and morality are trivialized by mass media, it is easier and easier for people to simply slip away as the church experience seems less and less relevant. Mass media teach children that religion is neither good nor bad. It simply doesn't matter.

On the other hand, those who choose as adults to become Catholics certainly know why they are here. Some came into the church as converts from other religious experiences, or perhaps from no religion at all. They do so through the Rite of Christian Initiation of Adults. They begin their walk of faith by studying and praying the Word of God each week, culminating with an intense retreat before the Easter Vigil. The movement in the church today is built upon the recognition that our ultimate goal is to *assist Catholics to become adults of deep faith*. Even the youth ministry model so often described in this book is aimed at teens, not just for their uniqueness as adolescents, but also as emerging adults, with the goal of providing a springboard to an adult faith.

Youth Ministry built a model of faith development for adolescents around the Emmaus encounter (Luke 24). (See Chapter 14.) The primary characteristics were peer ministry, listening, prayer, readiness, invitation, and commitment. Just as so many programmatic aspects of youth ministry from the 1970s and '80s were later adopted by broader pastoral ministry, that plan for faith development seems equally applicable in today's adult church. For instance, peer ministry is not uniquely applicable to teens. It is equally appropriate to adults. People of all ages can benefit from hearing the stories of others just like them.

The three sequential components of that model are evangelization, catechesis, and ministry. (Apologies if my definitions of these three words and yours don't quite match. Trust me. Go with the flow for the moment and hope that it all makes sense.) First, look at how our bishops define adult faith development.

In *Our Hearts Were Burning Within Us*, our bishops presented a plan for "a new focus on adult faith formation." Our work, they suggested, should strive to:

- Help each person to deepen their relationship with Jesus,

- Help each person to grow in their faith and hold on to the excitement brought about through that moment of personal conversion,

- Help each person to commit to works of service as a response to these new convictions,

- Help each person to begin or intensify a daily prayer life,

- Help each person to reach out to and invite others to share this experience,

- And, as each person walks the walk with others, help each person to repeat the process over and over, deeper and deeper each time.

Now, compare the steps offered by the U. S. Bishops to those described below and you will see remarkable similarities—just slightly different words. Both descriptions provide opportunities for personal conversion, followed by lifelong catechesis and moving to ministry. **The church is making a big shift in its thinking—moving from a *presumption of faith to opportunities for conversion*, and moving from transmission of the teachings of the church *to children* to lifelong formation and catechesis *of adults*. It goes even further, however. Our bishops are challenging us to make adult faith the central task in our catechetical enterprise—the central task, essentially superseding the large programs for children that most parishes presently have—not replacing the programs for children, but becoming a priority among parish priorities.**

■ Evangelization

"Evangelize" is a word that Catholics run from because they have images of 1-800 numbers to call with their credit card pledges, or Jimmy Swaggart with tears in his eyes and a Bible in his hands. Evangelization means taking your beliefs into the world. It is in the world that religious values are lived out, in places priests never get to, in the factories and offices and shops where you work, to your life outside the church building, where people are. The eleven Apostles streamed out of the upper room following their moment of encounter with the Holy Spirit and shouted in many languages to all to recognize Jesus as the Risen Lord. Imagine the impact when these men poured into the streets and shared their experiences with their peers. After two thousand years, evangelization still works the same way! *Evangelization comes first.*

NB.!

When evangelization takes place, we hear stories of conversion—not conversion *to* Catholicism, but *within* Catholicism—helping Catholics move through conversion to catechesis and beyond, moving Catholics from being Mass-goers to being parishioners. This is the kind of evangelization covered in this chapter. It is the kind of evangelization that has the greatest urgency. (A broader evangelization, or outreach to the un-churched, is covered in Chapter 16.)

Evangelization means the proclamation of the Gospel (as distinct from its explanation). Great parishes offer evangelization retreats, perhaps on Saturday and Sunday afternoon, perhaps on a series of evenings, where people can move to a closer relationship with God. Many will choose to join Small Christian Communities. (See Chapter 18.) Great parishes evangelize with relevant Sunday homilies that link faith to real life, access to retreats like the Cursillo, and programs on Tuesday evenings or Sunday afternoons akin to traditional parish missions. Great parishes realize that they must provide many different entry points to accommodate different needs.

Always remember that one person's personal experience trying to deal with life, faith, moral decision making, and God is incredibly moving to another in the same boat. That is peer-to-peer ministry. Most effective evangelization experiences are built upon this premise.

At one parish, the seventh- and eighth-grade students were participating in a retreat. A speaker on the retreat, a young man in high school only a few years older, spoke to them about sex and drugs and the choices that he (and they) must make each day of their lives. He spared nothing. He talked about HIV and drug abuse and peer pressure and virginity and temptations. He spoke of his faith and his own journey, which had many peaks and valleys. I watched the students. They were riveted to his every word. Do you think that they would have listened to you or me talk about virginity? They listened to him! Peer ministry works. Peer ministry is effective, whether teen to teen, or forty-year-old to forty-year-old, or eighty-year-old to eighty-year-old. Peer ministry is at the heart of the faith development process.

There comes a time when the person in this stage of faith development has a moment of recognition, a point of decision, a personal "Aha!" moment. Until this instant, faith development has become stagnant or stopped, or perhaps has even been rejected, because the person has seen it as a muddy blend of external doctrines and quaint, irrelevant practices. But now, following this conversion, the person finds faith beautiful and worth pursuing. *There comes a natural desire to want to learn more about it: catechesis.* Catechesis can't come first; it must follow evangelization. First comes the proclamation of the Word, then comes its explanation.

◼ Catechesis

As personal commitments to draw closer to Jesus are made, great parishes offer opportunities for both faith growth and ongoing adult education to provide a pastorally and theologically well-founded basis for faith and then for ministry. Do not presume that the catechetical effort toward children will be abandoned. On the contrary, the goal is a program that reaches every member of the parish.

Great parishes offer ongoing opportunities for these persons to continue to process, understand, and sort out the changes that have happened to them, helping them to develop a richer understanding of faith. Growth in faith comes through continued sharing in prayer and reflection with others along the same journey.

They also take their members through the teachings of the Catholic Church. They help them to integrate these teachings into their lives. We have all heard the criticism that the church is full of "buffet" or "cafeteria" Catholics, those who pick and choose which teachings they will accept and those they will ignore. Members learn the fundamentals; they learn the vocabulary. But understanding the doctrines of the church is not enough. They also need to understand how to live their faith every day as Christians. Through the combination, then, of faith development and adult education, they acquire a greater comfort level and confidence talking about it with one another. Examples of catechesis are small groups within the parish where individual needs can be met, bringing components of formation and education into the many organizations already active in the parish, programs that connect faith to real life, and others that move beyond an understanding of doctrine to a commitment to discipleship. *Then, they can live it out: ministry.*

■ Ministry

This is where prayer is even more important. It helps us move from volunteerism to ministry, from seeing our work as task, or something nice to do, to seeing it as the faith response to our calling from God. It seems an almost natural and automatic sequence of stages: The person first hears the Word of God, is touched by the Word, has a personal moment of recognition, delves more deeply into the meaning of the Word in one's life, and then wants to share this experience with others. Examples of ministry are everywhere in the parish; ministers of hospitality, of welcome, of religious education, of music, of administration. Every great parish offers countless opportunities for service, for ministry. One pastor always speaks of the pastoral year, never the fiscal year. Such a subtle change as this gently tells parishioners that ministry is the issue here, not finances.

■ Relationships—The Heart of Ministry

Youth ministry and adult faith development are both built upon personal relationships of *trust*. It happens after one person hears the story of another's faith journey, and then trusts in the integrity of that person, a peer. It is only then that an openness to the message of Jesus begins to occur. It is only then that the recipient can put away all the old cynicism about the church and believe in the genuineness of the invitation for them to become more deeply a part of the community of faith.

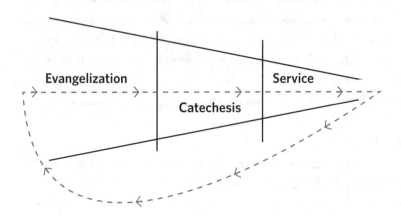

This model of faith development was originally called the "wedge" model, because the number of persons in each category tended to become smaller. Starting with an invitation to hospitality, some will respond and participate in the community. A few will experience moments of recognition and look for a deeper understanding of faith. Still fewer will move further into service and ministry to others. "Many are called but few are chosen" (Matthew 22:14). For those who do move deeply though faith, it is imperative that the parish offer training in leadership development and peer ministry.

This is how people move from being Mass-goers to parishioners to ministers. It is the essential role of the Catholic parish and all of its ministers to provide the settings where this movement can happen. "Providing the setting" is a phrase literally loaded with implications, because human beings don't respond to a "setting." People respond to other people. They say "Yes" when they are invited, when they become involved and feel connected. They say "Yes" when this process is natural and authentic and comes from the heart. The greatest challenge of this plan is translating "settings" into real people on their own journeys who are waiting to share their stories with others. It doesn't mean a parish church filled with saints. It means a community of believers on their own journeys of faith willing to invite others to walk with them—peer ministry.

This also means that the parish must constantly offer many different opportunities for persons at all stages of faith development. After all, the people of the parish will not, as one large group, move from evangelization to catechesis to ministry. The model is built upon readiness, and the parish must be prepared and equipped to assist each person at their stage of that process, with many different opportunities to begin (or continue) the journey.

It doesn't stop there, though. This model of faith development is actually circular, always looping around and starting over. Over and over, we continue to deepen our faith. We never "graduate." Each time we become ministers and help another person walk his or her own journey, we continually move deeper and deeper in our own faith, and come to understand it to be the work of our entire lifetime.

Remember: God is playing a great big joke on all of us super-organized, result-driven leaders. The changes we seek assist parishioners in their own personal faith development, their own conversion, if you will. The joke is that we can't see the results of this work. We can't see someone's conversion. We can only see some outward signs that something good is happening. How do we know that it is working? Don't look for a new crop of halos, or tongues of flame. God works much more subtly than that. There are no visible benchmarks, but leaders will begin to get intuitive hunches. Remember: We are talking about the faith development of those already in the parish.

Look for some of these signs of change:

- Meetings of leadership groups (pastoral council, etc.) begin to take on a warmer, more conciliatory tone, with more signs of love, flexibility, fewer "Gotcha!" moments, reduced conflict, and acceptance of different viewpoints. (I know; I can't wait, either!)

- More evidence of hospitality toward others, and an openness to reach out to visitors.

- More members show a greater generosity in sharing their gifts of time, of talent, and of treasure. When parishioners are happy with their church, they may have a renewed enthusiasm and are more inclined to seek ways to deepen their involvement with it and to say, "Thank you."

- A new awareness of the need to reach out to the poor. In one parish, this manifested itself by a reaching out to the homeless man who slept in the back of the church instead of shooing him out.

- A deepening sense of community and belonging. This can be very elusive.

- A call for more opportunities to share prayer together. This might be seen through the enthusiasm with which parish group and committee meetings use reflection on Sunday's readings as their prayer.

- Sunday liturgies show more involvement, more love! The assembly seems to have more life to it.

- While it is a very subtle issue, ownership of the parish by parishioners will increase.

- And, yes, collections often go up.

- Finally, when parishioners begin to ask for more opportunities to deepen their faith, you will *know* that the Holy Spirit is truly at work in your church!

Overall, you will know that something has changed. The parish begins to show a new vitality.

◼ A Personal Story

Some years ago, I received a telephone call from someone representing a group called "Jesus California Style." (A Google search on that term doesn't produce any hits, so perhaps they no longer exist.) She asked me to make an appearance at a large revival-style rally that they were holding at the California Fair Grounds in Sacramento. The individual described the event and what they wanted of me. They wanted the Catholic perspective, having heard of our successes with the Emmaus program and the wedge model of faith development. Her description was full of evangelical jargon. She explained that I would speak right after Pat Boone. Gulp!

After listening carefully, I asked, "Are you sure you have the right person?" While I do a lot of public speaking, I don't sing any songs. I have a pretty straightforward talking style. I was torn between delight with the opportunity to share our experience with an entirely new audience and worry that they had me confused with someone else. (I still think to this day that they wanted Richard Reichert and not Jim Reinhardt.) "No, no," she assured me, "You're the person we want." I nervously agreed to speak.

Some months went by, and the fateful day arrived. I asked Andrea, a colleague, to go with me for moral support. As is usually the case when I am addressing a totally new group, I arrived early to scope out the scene and get an idea of what I was in for. I listened to Terry Bradshaw, the NFL commentator, tell his story of conversion. I watched various soloists, usually accompanied by slick, professionally produced recorded music, entertain the group—about ten thousand were there—with their witness talks and their songs. I chuckled through the performance by a young man with a puppet as he shared his (their?) experience of finding Jesus. Pat Boone emerged, as if on a cloud, from his air-conditioned Cadillac limo with smoky windows, dressed in a white suit, to dazzle everyone with entertainment and reassuring words. Later, as he returned to the cool comfort of his limo and disappeared into the distance, I turned to Andrea with great nervousness.

"What have I gotten myself into?" I asked. "Reinhardt," she said, "just go out there and tell them the truth. They may never hear this message from anyone else." Fortified by her encouraging words, with Bible in hand, I walked out onto the gigantic stage. It seemed like an acre in size!

I told them that I didn't sing or dance. I had no props. I had no accompaniment. What I did have was a story to tell them, a story about a part of the church with which they probably did not come into much contact, the Catholic part. I shared scriptural references that supported the wedge model. I talked about the importance of the parish for Catholics as the place where it happens. I challenged them to make this happen in their local churches. "After all," I asked gingerly, "how many weekend rallies or revivals can you attend? Don't you ultimately have to find a place for yourself in your own church?" The murmuring in the crowd suggested that this last question had pushed a lot of buttons. After forty minutes alone on a very large stage, I thanked them for listening, invited them to reflect upon our different experiences, and walked off to polite applause.

I was never invited back.

I tell this story because I firmly believe that the Catholic experience is rooted in the life of the parish. Ours is not an experience of revivals. We find Jesus most often through our encounters with one another in our local church. While some of us may go off for a Cursillo retreat or a Marriage Encounter or a Teens Encounter Christ weekend, we are always challenged to bring that experience back to our parishes and share it with our friends there. The parish is the locus of faith development in the Catholic Church. To paraphrase a quotation found in an entirely different context, "Church camp can be a valuable component in faith development, but it is up to the community of faith [the parish] to carry its meaning and relevance."

THE BIG QUESTIONS

In order for systemic change to happen, it's necessary to start with parish leaders. This is not to say that pastoral council members are not religious. It is to say that the faith development process is circular and built upon peer ministry. Consequently, starting with known leaders—the staff, the pastoral council, and all ministry leaders—will develop the peer ministers who will be so necessary for faith growth to spread. The big questions, then, are these.

How can you move task-oriented council members with full agendas into a new model of church? Conversion doesn't fit very well with tight schedules. It's mixing processes with programs.

How can you get a real commitment from these people, some of whom might have come into their roles for reasons having to do with their secular skills more than their faith?

Check out www.pastoralcouncils.com for some direction.

BIBLIOGRAPHY AND ASSOCIATED RESOURCES

Our Hearts Were Burning Within Us is a pastoral letter written by the U.S. bishops in 1999. Copies may be purchased from the publishing office of the U.S. Conference of Catholic Bishops at www.usccbpublishing.org.

The Pastoral Center (www.pastoralplanning.com), which is now partnered with Twenty-Third Publications, offers a rich source of material for life-long faith development in the parish. Bill Huebsch, who leads pastoral-planning.com, places faith development at the heart of all parish activity and, thus, approaches it as the foundational element of all parish planning. He is certainly one of the two pre-eminent writers on the subject of adult faith formation today.

The other is John Roberto, who founded the Center for Ministry Development. John is now also associated with this group and adds an even richer dimension to their work.

Parish Pastoral Councils (www.pastoralcouncils.com) paints a wonderful vision for what these groups ought to be.

The "Wedge Model" of ministry was originally developed in California in the 1970s and was used by the Norcal Youth Ministry Board members for many years. It was widely taught in youth ministry workshops throughout the U.S. Michael Warren and Tom Zanzig later wrote about it, but I have not found anything still in print on this approach.

CHAPTER 4

Who "Owns" the Parish?

So Jesus called them and said to them, "You know that among the Gentiles those whom they recognize as their rulers lord it over them, and their great ones are tyrants over them. But it is not so among you; but whoever wishes to become great among you must be your servant, and whoever wishes to be first among you must be slave of all. For the Son of Man came not to be served but to serve, and to give his life a ransom for many."

Mark 10:42–45

How do we turn the power pyramid upside down and move toward servant leadership? While we need nothing more than the words of Jesus himself to guide us toward the solution to this challenge, we can also look to significant contemporary authors for additional reflections. First, I can share my own personal experience.

■ A Personal Story

In my first professional job out of college, I worked in the home office of a large Midwestern life insurance company, in the Underwriting

Department. Because we were responsible for evaluating the insurability of every applicant and sometimes had to decline coverage, the relationship with the sales agents could occasionally become contentious. I had never before worked in a commercial enterprise, having been employed all during high school and college at the local YMCA. As a result, I had to learn the corporate culture to become effective.

It's amazing how God provides, even in a life insurance company. The woman who was my supervisor (I'll call her Barbara) taught me over the seven years of my employment there everything I know today about how to work with people, and how to supervise them. Barbara taught me that the key to successful leadership is a sense of service. She taught me that each of us needed to do everything possible to make our entire department succeed. I would succeed, she said, when we all succeeded. She taught me that even when others treated the field agents as enemies, we should treat them as colleagues. When they succeeded, we would succeed. She taught me that compassion and flexibility in the workplace made us better than competition and rigidity. She also taught all of us that playing together as a work team when we were off duty made us even better when we were on duty. She taught us all these things by the way she went about her daily duties, never by preaching. I didn't discover Robert Greenleaf's book *Servant Leadership* until several years after I left that company, but I later came to realize that she practiced it even if she didn't call it that.

Barbara is retired now. She and I have been lifelong friends. I owe more to her than to anyone other than my parents. I thank God for her presence in my life.

■ Turning the Power Pyramid Upside Down— Servant Leadership

In the 1970s, Robert K. Greenleaf wrote a book called *Servant Leadership*. He didn't write it as a religious man. It was not filled with theological jargon. He wrote it because he knew that it worked. He had spent a lifetime with AT&T, where he came to realize that traditional power models didn't work or, at the very least, were inappropriate. After he retired from AT&T, the success he experienced with his book spawned a new career teaching this radical management concept. In fact, he founded the Greenleaf Center for Servant Leadership and was associated with it until his death in 1990. It still exists and thrives today. Greenleaf himself went on to author move than twenty books, some of which apply directly to religious persons and institutions, while literally hundreds of books by other authors have been written on this subject.

Greenleaf first described a different way of thinking for the individual person.

> The servant-leader *is* servant first....It begins with the natural feeling that one wants to serve, to serve *first*. Then conscious choice brings one to aspire to lead. That person is sharply different from one who is **leader** first, perhaps because of the need to assuage an unusual power drive or to acquire material possessions....The leader-first and the servant-first are two extreme types. Between them there are shadings and blends that are part of the infinite variety of human nature.
>
> The difference manifests itself in the care taken by the servant-first to make sure that other people's highest priority needs are being served. The best test, and difficult to administer, is: Do those served grow as persons? Do they, *while being served*, become healthier, wiser, freer, more autonomous, more likely themselves to become servants? *And*, what is the effect on the least privileged in society; will they benefit, or, at least, not be further deprived?
>
> Robert K. Greenleaf, *The Servant as Leader*

Greenleaf went on to discuss how this phenomenon manifests itself within an organization.

> This is my thesis: **caring for persons, the more able and the less able serving each other, is the rock upon which a good society is built**. Whereas, until recently, caring was largely person to person, now most of it is mediated through institutions—often large, complex, powerful, impersonal; not always competent; sometimes corrupt. If a better society is to be built, one that is more just and more loving, one that provides greater creative opportunity for its people, then the most open course is to raise both the capacity to serve and the very performance as servant of existing major institutions by new regenerative forces operating within them.
>
> Robert K. Greenleaf, *The Institution as Servant*

The most fascinating aspect of his concept is that it is written almost entirely as a successful approach to leadership or management in the profit-making world. It is at the same time both pragmatic and altruistic. He espouses servant leadership because *it is the right thing to do* and because *it works*! In several of his writings, Greenleaf certainly acknowledges that it is consistent with religious morality, but that is not his main point. His message is that it makes business sense.

These two aspects, the individual and the institution as servant leader, are described below.

■ Traits of a Servant Leader

Servant leadership in the person is manifested through an amalgam of many different characteristics, some learned, some inherent. Some people are gifted with servant leadership as a natural way of being. Others need to develop certain qualities intentionally. For most all servant leaders, fully developing their leadership approach will be a lifelong process.

We Are Called

Jesus doesn't wait for volunteers. He calls each of us to a particular ministry. (See Chapter 7 for an elaboration of this theme.) Sometimes they hear this calling through an explicit invitation from a pastor or other ministry leader in their church. A few hear it directly from Our Lord. However it comes, if they are listening, they will know that they have been called.

Becoming a Listener

Listening to others, listening to our own inner voice, listening to God. Listening comes when one stops talking, when one is silent. It is coupled with reflection. The world we live in places little value on silence and listening. It is a task that requires cultivating and conscious attention.

The Gift of Empathy

Empathy is perhaps more of a quality than a skill. People just seem to know that certain individuals will appreciate what they are going through. Some people seem to have been gifted with empathy, while others will find it difficult to learn.

The Healing Process

When crises occur, some people not only understand, they help others find answers to move on. Others look to these people when the emotional need arises.

Awareness

Some people possess a particularly sharp sense of what is happening within themselves and all around them. They easily pick up on cues and signals everywhere to help form their views. They are not easily fooled by outward appearances. They understand their own gifts and talents and have a keen ability to see those of people around them. Because of this awareness, they form teams that work well together and support one another.

The Power of Persuasion

They rely upon their influence, point of view, and compelling reasoning over power or authority to move others. Being persuasive is very natural to them. Using force is never an option.

The Creative Process—Making Dreams Become Reality

They dream great dreams and are able to make an "Aha!" moment move to real results. Never just idea people, they have the ability to see an idea through from its spark through its execution.

Seeing the Future

If we fail to learn from the mistakes of the past, we are doomed to repeat them. Such leaders learn from the past, understand the present reality, and see the future. They easily pick up on patterns around them and read where they move. They can foresee consequences.

Being a Steward

They naturally nurture the resources of a group or organization, whether they be human, material, or otherwise. They cherish the organization's values and understand how to get results with them.

Personal Growth

When we minister to others and foster their growth, we grow as persons ourselves. The Chinese sage Lao Tzu wrote the *Tao Te Ching*, a treatise on what would ultimately be called servant leadership: "The greatest leader forgets himself and attends to the development of others." Perhaps there is nothing new under the sun.

Building Community

No man is an island. We are never alone in this world. We are called to community. How do we foster and encourage it? How are we facilitators of community in our lives and in our church?

■ Re-Inventing the Wheel

The Present Reality

What happens when our parish changes? Let me use my present parish, the Church of the Epiphany in San Francisco, as a case in point.

San Francisco is a city composed of very distinctive neighborhoods, each with its own different personality. Epiphany is located in the Excelsior District, what some would call the Outer Mission District. Epiphany was founded and built by the Irish and Italians in the 1920s. Following World War II, large numbers of Hispanics moved into the Mission District, giving it the extraordinary Latin flavor it still has today. Beginning in the 1970s, Filipinos and Pacific Islanders moved into the Excelsior. All these groups came with large Catholic populations. Meanwhile, lots of other ethnic groups with smaller Catholic populations did the same. Of course, the Irish and Italians didn't disappear. While their numbers have diminished through time, they are still there and represent a disproportionate number of the seniors of the parish. The Mission District is still dominated by Hispanic numbers, and Filipinos continue to arrive in large numbers. Epiphany is like the United Nations! One of the most successful social events of the year is International Night, with food from everywhere.

Epiphany has changed many times, essentially re-inventing itself as each group made its presence known, bringing its own different rich tradition of food, language, socializing, music, expressing their faith in God, and celebrating life. Building bridges between groups to foster harmony and understanding became a major task of the last three pastors. Epiphany is like many parishes across the United States. Our country continues to change, and so do our parishes.

One constant exists with all organizations, whether large or small: Each time it changes, it must redefine itself. This is true for small prayer groups, for large parishes, and for our country. Does this mean that we who hold the power, in our generosity, invite these others to join our parish? However politely expressed, usually said with a smile, this can be interpreted as "It's our way or the highway. Take it or leave it. We were here first." Or does it mean that all of us, all stakeholders, old and new, must sit around the same table and re-decide what our parish is about? Everyone gets a vote. Just when you think you know where you're going, you have to start over and reset your direction. This is never easy. It's messy. It's time-consuming. It's usually painful for existing members. And, it's not efficient. It is however, the right thing to do.

It is certainly true for our nation. We see the signs of stress all around us. Battles about immigration, day laborers, one official language, and going to the back of the line, sometimes seemingly tinged with racism, never go away. It's worth being regularly reminded that everyone in America (except Native Americans) was at one time an immigrant, a newcomer to this country. All of us, or our ancestors, had to find a place for ourselves. On a national level, American history is full of conflicted moments when those already here were reluctant to make room for those just arriving.

If you know the stories of your ancestors' arrival in America, you may be keenly aware of the struggles experienced by your own forebears. It might have happened to you, or your parents, or to your ancestors several generations ago, but it almost certainly happened. It happened to the Irish, the Germans, the Poles, Puerto Ricans, the Chinese, Eastern Europeans, Mexicans, Vietnamese, Latin Americans, Pacific Islanders, Filipinos, and probably every other ethnic group that migrated to the U. S. at one time or another. As democratic as we claim to be, it seems to be part of our human nature to be just a bit selfish. We don't want to let go of what we already have, what we worked so hard to achieve, what we earned.

Oh, and by the way, this isn't just an American problem. I was in Berlin in 1990, just months after the Wall came down. My taxi driver spoke with derision of the lower status of the East Germans

("They aren't as smart as we Westerners") and the Turks ("We hire the Turks do all our menial tasks"). Doesn't that sound familiar?

■ Re-Inventing Your Parish

To share power authentically, we must first understand one another and put aside fears, suspicions and distrust that come with different accents, languages, ways of worshipping, ways of dressing, and the like. Most of us relish the status quo, *our* status quo. Accepting change is usually easier in small doses.

Each new generation of Catholics—from wherever they come in the world—must ask the same questions about their place in the world, and in the parish, over and over again. It does no good for those of us already here, those who asked these questions ourselves, to say "We know the answers. We've been there, done that. Listen to us." **Each new group must discover the answers to those questions themselves. The challenge is that sometimes those answers will be the same as the ones earlier discovered, but sometimes they will be different.**

The challenge for a servant parish is to keep re-inventing itself so that it more authentically reflects the realities of all its members. Doing this will probably take a long time with many steps. Here are some.

- Bring in an outside group facilitator to direct initial steps in the process, where the goal is to really get to know one another. Such a person brings both a neutrality of position, with no hidden agenda, and a skill set in directing group process activities around this issue that the pastor might not have.

- If your diocese has an office of ethnic ministries, invite staff from appropriate ones to visit your parish to help your leadership understand different cultures. If no such office or service exists, look to neighboring parishes that have experienced the same kind of change. Ask some of their leadership to visit with you and share their stories.

- Look at particular ethnic cultural centers for this kind of help. While not exclusively church-directed, they know, understand and advocate for their group. They know the important issues.

- Host your own International Dinner. Food and music and dance and dress from different places make for a joyful noise!

- Recognize that different languages will be present with newly arrived immigrant groups. Many from these countries will tell you that English is not always an easy language to learn. So many synonyms from so many different languages that hold subtly different nuances of meaning. So many idiomatic expressions steeped in American lore. Try explaining the expression "happy as a pig in a poke" to someone from China who speaks little English. So many variations on rules of pronunciation that seem to make no sense whatsoever—they're just there. Offer English as a Second Language classes for new parishioners.

- While your parish may already offer eucharistic celebrations in different languages, like a Spanish Mass, try also to bring different cultural expressions into the mainstream language Mass. English speakers need to get used to different ways that different people celebrate the Eucharist.

This is by no means a complete list. If your members have an openness to change, you will discover your own set of steps that you need to take.

Let me restate and slightly modify a previous point. It isn't just the amalgam of villages that makes San Francisco a great city. It is the openness of all San Franciscans to accept that each village is a little different from theirs, Accepting those differences, one village from another, is what makes San Francisco a great city. Accepting those differences will help to make your parish a great one as well.

■ The Tables Are Turned!

There was a time, one or two generations ago, when pastors used the following rule of thumb: About two-thirds of the parishioners would be involved in the life of the parish and the other one-third either coasted or were invisible. In little more than one generation those fractions have essentially become reversed! Three recent studies document this new reality.

U.S. Religious Landscape Survey

The Pew Forum on Religion & Public Life released the findings of this study, based on interviews with more than 35,000 Americans in late 2007. They found that, of major Christian denominations, the Catholic Church had lost the greatest number of people to changes in affiliation. About one-third of those surveyed who had been raised Catholic said they no longer identified as such. The survey pointed out that some move to other religious groups while others continue with a private religious life with no affiliation connection. Once again the private "Me and God" approach shows itself.

When questioned further, those who left the Church felt that the faith expression it offered was impersonal. They tended to join religions that offered better opportunities for involvement and engagement, usually in smaller churches.

Like the Trinity College study reported below, the Pew study found that the Catholic Church had held relatively steady in its numbers, due primarily to the immigration of predominantly Catholic populations, such as Latin Americans, which successfully offset the numbers of those leaving the church. The impact of this reality is that the Catholic Church in the United States will soon become an overwhelmingly Hispanic one. This change is already quite apparent in California and other Southwestern states.

American Religious Identification Survey

In March 2009, Trinity College of Hartford, Connecticut, released its third "American Religious Identification Survey," covering nearly 55,000 U.S. adults. Many diocesan newspapers reported its findings. Some of its conclusions were relatively obvious, only confirming what many Catholic leaders already knew.

- Catholic numbers were growing most in the U.S. Southwest, with its increasing number of Mexicans and Latin Americans. California has a higher percentage of Catholics than New England.

- The numbers of Catholics in the Northeast were down.

- The number of U.S. residents claiming no religious affiliation had gone up significantly, from 8.2% in 1990 to 14.2% in 2001 to 15% in 2008.

- The percentage of adults claiming to be Christian dropped from more than eighty-six percent in 1990 to seventy-six percent in 2008.

- While the number of U.S. adults claiming to be Catholic had actually increased (to fifty-seven million), that increase had not kept up with the overall population increase. The percentage of Catholics had actually dropped one point to twenty-five percent since 1990.

- Mainline Protestants suffered a 10% reduction in numbers, while *Evangelical or Born Again groups experienced a 295% increase.*

One analyst pointed out that declines in church affiliation are more a result of "generational replacement" than "individual loss of identity," meaning that as older religiously affiliated persons die, they are replaced by younger persons claiming no affiliation. Parishes certainly see this among young people, and at a rate that seems to be accelerating. Anecdotal evidence from young people suggests that they find their religious experience through a "Me and God" approach, constructing an amalgam of beliefs, however altruistic, that suits the individual and doesn't particularly represent those of one organized religious group.

Gallup Polls

In April 2009, the Gallup Organization released findings about church attendance. It claims that Protestant weekly attendance has remained basically steady for sixty years, ranging from forty-two percent in 1955 to forty-five percent in the mid-2000s. Catholic Mass attendance during the same period has *dropped from seventy-five percent to forty-five percent*, to where it now matches the Protestant level. The attendance numbers for Catholic young adults (in their twenties) have dropped even more, to thirty percent.

Another Gallup survey found that thirty-two percent of Catholics describe themselves as "engaged" with their parish, fifty-two percent "uninvolved," and sixteen percent "actively disengaged."

These findings are very grim indeed.

THE BIG QUESTIONS

As Catholics, we live with a certain paradox. All members of leadership in the parish—not just the pastor—should share the ownership of the decisions of the parish, but the church is not built upon a democratic model. Each pastor has the opportunity to expand parish leadership and involve everyone in its direction and programs both by becoming a servant leader himself and by the way he builds inclusive leadership structures around him. How, then, does your pastor do this? Is he by temperament built this way? Or is this an acquired skill? How can church members help this happen?

All the studies and surveys point to growth in small, personal churches and stagnation in big, institutional ones. If your church is large, what must you do to break down the walls of depersonalization that may be present there? If your church is small, what steps must you take to strengthen the personal experiences that your members probably already have?

BIBLIOGRAPHY AND ASSOCIATED RESOURCES

Check out the Greenleaf Center for Servant Leadership (www.greenleaf.org) for any of Robert Greenleaf's publications. This concept has become a movement, still very dynamic and vital, with frequent periodicals and workshops. His list of the traits of a servant leader appear in nearly all his books, although they are frequently modified for the particular audience.

Greenleaf, Robert K., *Servant Leadership: A Journey into the Nature of Legitimate Power and Greatness.*

The Servant as Leader, published by the Greenleaf Center.

The Institution As Servant, published by the Greenleaf Center, but now out of print.

Keith, Dr. Kent M., *The Case for Servant Leadership*, published by the Greenleaf Center. In this short book, Dr. Keith, CEO of the Center, makes the case that "servant leadership is ethical, practical, and meaningful."

The Pew Forum on Religion and Public Life (www.pewforum.org) published the findings of a study that they called the "U.S. Religious Landscape Survey." Check them out for more detail on this reference.

In March 2009, Trinity College of Hartford, Connecticut, released its third "American Religious Identification Survey." For more information, go to www.americanreligionsurvey-aris.org.

Although not cited in this book, William D'Antonio of Catholic University of America has also written extensively on the condition of the American Catholic Church. See *American Catholics Today: New Realities of Their Faith and Their Church*, Rowman & Littlefield, 2007.

Frank Donaldson, President of The Institute of School and Parish Development (www.ispd.com) and its principal author, writes frequently of Gallup studies. While his company's title might suggest fundraising, his principal emphasis is on making the parish great and encouraging lifelong faith development. He is absolutely right on target on this subject and **his Web site is probably the single most valuable resource I can recommend in this book!** Get on the mailing list for their e-mail newsletters, particularly for Catholic development. (They also emphasize Catholic school enrollment management.)

CHAPTER 5

Must We Talk about Money?
Understand Stewardship

Almighty and ever faithful Lord, gratefully acknowledging your mercy and humbly admitting our need, we pledge our trust in You and in each other. Filled with desire, we respond to your call for discipleship by shaping our lives in imitation of Christ. We profess the call that requires us to be stewards of your gifts. As stewards, we receive your gifts gratefully, we cherish and tend them in a responsible manner, we share them in practice and love with others, and we return them with increase to the Lord. We pledge to our ongoing formation as stewards and our responsibility to call others to that same endeavor. Almighty and ever faithful God, it is our fervent hope and prayer that You who have begun this good work in us will bring it to fulfillment in Jesus Christ, the Lord. Amen.

From the Stewardship Office of the
Diocese of Colorado Springs, Colorado

Must we talk about money again? The answer is usually "No." Making a profit is not the principal goal of every parish activity. Community building and fellowship come first.

A pastor of a great parish spoke at a large stewardship conference. "Many people miss the point," he said. "They go right to the treasure part. They see the money our people give, and they want to take a shortcut right to it. It can't be done! They miss the fact that the people have to undergo a conversion to the stewardship way of life, which is gradual. People have to feel a sense of ownership of the parish. When they know it's theirs—not the priest's, not the bishop's—they want to give of themselves—in time, in talent, and then in treasure."

What I learned in the first ten seconds there: **"Of the three, treasure is way down the list. Work first on time and talent. Treasure will follow."** Stewardship has only a little to do with fundraising. People will give to a parish what it deserves, what it is worthy of. This will relate directly to the quality of its staff, its programs, the satisfaction level of its parishioners with its organizational processes, and, most important, *how they feel about belonging*. After all, you can only be a steward of what has been given to you. If it isn't "yours," then you're not likely to take care of it. This is true of all their gifts—time, talent, and treasure.

The title of this book has to do with great parishes. Some others speak of excellent parishes. Substitute the word "stewardship" for either "great" or "excellent." They all mean the same thing. Furthermore, it goes without saying that most big parishes got that way because they are so good. They become the center of life for many, many people. They develop the happy problem that too many people sign up for events instead of not enough. Let's examine these propositions.

For most people, stewardship probably means fundraising, increasing the collection, or perhaps caring for the parish or serving on committees. Over the years, they've heard countless homilies on these themes. The pastor brings in a speaker from the diocesan office on "Stewardship Sunday," but the punch line of his talk is always to increase the offerings. In recent years, they broadened the definition to include the now familiar "time, talent, and treasure." Too often, though, it still seemed to be camouflage for getting more money.

Now, a new movement has emerged which calls upon us to go through a change in thinking—about being Catholic, about the meaning of our baptism, and about the church. Clearly, stewardship is more about our gifts of time and talent than our gift of treasure. The definition is still a bit fuzzy and is described differently by different authors. Here are some definitions:

1. Stewardship is a spirituality based upon our gratitude for all God's gifts.

2. It is a biblical directive to treat all of our abilities, our good fortune and our material means as gifts from God.

3. Stewardship becomes the pastoral foundation for everything that happens in the parish.

4. The U.S. Catholic Bishops offered a pastoral letter titled *Stewardship: A Disciple's Response*, that defined it as "our recognition that everything we have has been given by God—our time, our talent, our money, yes even life itself."

5. John Westerhoff, a popular Christian writer, describes it as "everything we do after we say we believe." (I like this one best.)

Making gratitude to God the foundation of parish life, and by extension, my own life, requires a kind of humility that can be difficult to accept, especially for anyone having that All-American "can do" attitude. It's easy to forget that we are not entirely responsible for our own successes.

The U.S. bishops spoke of an endlessly repeating stewardship cycle:

1. We receive God's gifts gratefully.

2. We cultivate them responsibly.

3. We share them lovingly in justice with others.

4. We return them with increase to the Lord.

And around it goes.

To repeat, this model of church requires a change in thinking about what it means to be Catholic. It challenges Mass-goers to become parishioners, parishioners to become ministers. Passive Catholics, those who simply meet their Sunday obligation (maybe), those with a "me and God" devotional life, those who are uncomfortable with sharing, will find this new way of thinking very challenging. Going back to the "three Ts," the focus has moved to "time and talent," with the full conviction that "treasure" will follow.

Pastorally, we are called upon to rethink the meaning of our own baptism as well. The Sacraments of Initiation—baptism, confirmation and Eucharist—all call us to lives of service to others, lives of giving. **We sometimes forget that our commitment to service comes from baptism, not ordination**; or perhaps we missed it in catechism class.

The key part of Westerhoff's definition is "after we say we believe." It is all that "doing," all that ownership, by so many parishioners sensitized to this new way of thinking that gradually makes a parish great. There are some identifiable characteristics of a great parish.

- Just as great cities are amalgams of neighborhoods, so too are great parishes. New York City is that way. So are Paris, France and San Francisco. Your city may be, too. Each is made of many unique, vibrant, identifiable neighborhoods.

Parisians call theirs villages. Life in the St. Germain quarter is lived one way, and it's different from Belleville, or the Batignolles, or the Marais. Each is a little different. But together they make a wonderful whole. No Parisian would ever think that they should all become the same. People in these neighborhoods all boast of being Parisians, but they all express it a bit differently. Great parishes are like that, too. They don't try to homogenize all groups into one. Instead, they acknowledge and encourage their many different approaches to life and ways in which they express their faith in God. They break down the anonymity of a large church and address the needs of people (and peoples). Just as when the circus comes to town, the parish is a big tent under which many groups can gather. It makes for a joyful noise!

- In Chapter 2, the case was made that prayer must be at the center of a great parish. Great parishes are beehives of activity, but spirituality is the foundation for all things. Prayer is at the center of all meetings and groups; not rote, recited prayer, but shared, reflective, authentic prayer. A great parish is spiritually rich. It is a place where people can be close to God because they find opportunities to connect with God all around them. In addition, they find others who want to share that value. It is a place where, to repeat, it is easy to be good.

- Great parishes run over with compassion and warmth. Everyone knows that they are loved and cared for there. The community is the most important thing. It is the place where you know everyone and everyone knows you—or at least everyone is working to get to that point. It's a parish like the one in Schenectady, New York (described in the story in Chapter 14), where the people in my pew realized that I was a stranger and welcomed me. It's the place that I would turn

to if I were in trouble and needed to know that I could absolutely count on the person I was asking for help.

- Great parishes have *no volunteers*—I repeat, no volunteers—
but they have lots and lots of ministers. That's because Jesus
never waited for volunteers. He invited others to join him.
Over and over, he invited. That's the way of a great parish,
where life is built around everyone walking the walk of faith,
from evangelization, to catechesis, to ministry. (Chapter 7
covers this idea thoroughly.)

- Great parishes give countless entry points for people to
become involved, in a way that fits the moment. People
come to a parish from many places around the world, from
many different backgrounds, with many different gifts, and
with many different needs. Some people are joiners and
some aren't. Different people come to recognize the presence of the Lord in their lives at many different moments. A
great parish offers many ways for everyone to find a place at
the table—the Table of the Lord.

- People have fun in great parishes because they are places full
of welcome and hospitality. Everyone just loves to be there.
If you receive a warm welcome at the parish office, if they
know you by name, if the Sunday Mass is a rich time in your
week, with relevant homilies rooted in everyday experience,
joyful music, and a warm feeling of belonging, if religious
education is exciting, if you are proud to be in the buildings,
how could you not be happy being there?

When a person finds such a parish and is immersed in it, then
the natural next step is to join in more deeply to help others become
involved as well. (That process of movement through faith development was described more thoroughly back in Chapter 3.) This is
where the gifts of time and talent come in. In catechism class, Sister

taught us that the church is the body of Christ. If that is true, then our ongoing task is the further strengthening and building of that body. While we can obviously do that through our gifts of dollars (treasure), we can do it just as well through our gifts of prayer, involvement, and leadership (time and talent).

Every Catholic church and certainly every Catholic school lives through the involvement of its members. I shun the use of the word "volunteer" in favor of the more accurate "minister." No church or school survives without them. While the parish has a small paid staff (both ordained and lay), it usually has many times more parishioners who are actually the ones who make things happen: catechists, ushers, musicians, office helpers, group leaders, lectors, sacristans, and on and on. It's the same for the school: hot lunch helpers, envelope stuffers, yard aides, field trip drivers, Parent-Teacher Guild leaders, more office helpers, classroom aides. Add your own here. All these people share their gifts of time and talent. One of our tasks is to help them move from thinking of themselves as volunteers to realizing that they are ministers. This is part of the internal evangelizing that we need to do, and it will become a natural result of the faith development processes of the parish.

When a parish conducts a capital campaign, it asks members to pledge a gift of treasure. Parishioners are asked to complete pledge cards indicating the size of their gift and the terms and method of payment. They place their signature on the card as a visible sign of commitment, their promise to honor the pledge. Great parishes build upon that idea and ask members to offer pledges of time and talent as well. Many do this annually. These pledge cards are formalized and often list different opportunities for giving:

- Promises of Prayer, listing different ways to offer prayer for members to check.

- Promises of Involvement, describing the many ways that people can connect to the parish more completely.

- Promises of Talent, where they declare particular skills or hobbies that they can give to parish life.

Parishioners receive a "Time and Talent" brochure covering everything the parish does, and often what it wishes it could do. While this process can take place at a Sunday Mass, or a Town Hall Meeting, or a Ministry Fair, what if the parish could gather the people to do it personally, much in the way a capital campaign is conducted—one parishioner visiting another, sharing their own involvement in parish life, what that involvement has given back to them, and inviting another family to do the same? After all, if a family is only peripherally connected to the parish, they probably have never thought of what it takes to make parish life happen.

This process will help more members understand that all kinds of talents or gifts are needed to build the body of Christ. Perhaps theirs can fit into the mix as well. Great parishes find that once all three Ts, time, talent, and treasure, are given equal levels of importance, more members will be open to sharing what they have, even if money is not at the top of their list at that moment.

From the horror stories of other parishes. Here are some readily identifiable pitfalls around stewardship and its inherent values.

Are We Preaching to the Choir?

Do you confidently put announcements in the Sunday bulletin and then wonder why so few respond to them? And they're always the same people who do! Do the math and the answer will be clear. What is your typical weekend Mass count? How many individuals are represented by the families listed in the parish database? Do you reach twenty-five percent? Thirty percent? Regrettably, ice on the streets, or a dreary, rainy Sunday morning, or even an important NFL game in the early time slot can significantly reduce Mass attendance. And you're left with seventy percent or more of your parish that never sees the bulletin or hears the pulpit announcement. The lesson here is that if you communicate only rarely with the inactive members of the parish, they will remain inactive.

Too Much Talk About Money

Do they only hear from you when you want money? How many times have you heard that complaint? If the only piece of mail your inactive members receive is your Christmas appeal, why are you surprised when the percentage of responses is so tiny? Inactive members are inactive because they don't feel any sense of connection with the parish. Rightly or wrongly, something just isn't clicking for them. Inactive members are no more likely to donate to a church with whom they feel no relationship than they are to come to Mass. It doesn't take rocket science to figure this out.

Beware of Double Messages

If "stewardship" truly means "everything we do after we say we believe," then don't negate that definition by sending a double message with other pre-printed pieces, perhaps obtained from a third-party source, that say something else. In other words, don't let the pulpit message say one thing and real life in the parish say something else. Remember: For too many years the message on "Stewardship Sunday" was really about giving more money. Remember, too: If you do a Google search on "church stewardship," the majority of hits will have to do with fundraising services or consultants. If you are genuinely changing the definition, then you must be totally consistent. Examine everything that is mailed to parishioners or is said from the pulpit or appears in the bulletin to make certain that everyone is giving the same message.

Keep the Front Desk and the Back Desk in Sync

We've discussed it in other chapters, but the point is always worth repeating. Make certain that everyone in leadership in the parish (and the school) supports the same message. The pastor can preach peace, love, and good will every Sunday, but it is all for naught if the church sacristan gives an arriving funeral party a grumpy reception. Or if the front desk is staffed by a receptionist who had a bad night and shares it with each visitor. Or if a basketball coach throws a fit at a bad call in front of children and parents. The body of Christ is made of many parts, and each part must do its job in harmony with all the others. This is why evangelization must start at home, with the staff, with the key leaders and other ministers *who are the parish* to the many people with just passing involvement with the church.

We've all heard the cynical comments in conversations at the workplace and the coffee shop from those who have had bad experiences with a church. "That church is just a business." "All they want is my money." "The church is just a social club, and they don't care about anybody who isn't in it." "The church is hypocritical. Aren't they supposed to be perfect?"

We will never be able to silence all critics. There are some who, for whatever reason, simply will never accept the value and importance of the church. But we can work to make our church live out the values that it preaches. We aren't perfect. We have feet of clay. But we must work to make our church what it preaches to be. We do that first by starting with ourselves. And, yes, we do have God on our side.

■ How Do We Get There?

This is a tall order and won't happen overnight. It certainly can't be scripted ahead of time, but following these steps will begin to get you there. Remember: *A great parish is a stewardship parish is a great parish.* Do you have friends who have abandoned their tradi-

tional neighborhood parish for one in another part of town? Most
large cities have one. Sometimes, they are university churches or
campus ministry centers. Sometimes they are inner city parishes.
There isn't always a commonality here. They are sometimes called
"magnet" parishes, a title particularly apt because these parishes
seem to draw people to them. Take a moment to ask these friends
why they belong there. Listen to the characteristics of these parishes, and you will almost certainly find the kinds of places described
in this chapter. They probably speak of that parish being a place
where you feel welcome, whoever you are. A place where there are
no hoops to jump through, where the values we hold are real and
expressed every day.

It is good to remember that it is the parish where faith is lived.
While the Vatican is important—for, after all, we are a universal
church, not a congregational one—it is the parish that has the potential to touch each of our lives every day. The parish *is* the church
for most people—the place where the rubber meets the road. And,
of course, it is the parish that we have the opportunity and ability
to change. It probably goes without saying, then, that the better a
parish is, the more likely its members are to say "Thank you." That
is stewardship in action.

When stewardship is not a program, but a way of life or an underlying theology, then the question arises, "How do you do it?
How do you place stewardship at the center of parish life?" The
quick answer is, "Let's have a Stewardship Committee!" But where
does it fit in? Throughout the church, many different models are in
place, ranging from a stand-alone committee alongside other committees, to an oversight committee. Essentially, though, it serves the
same purpose as the pastoral council. Stewardship is not a program, but a concept that ought to be at the heart of everything that
happens in the parish. Perhaps the best answer is that a key role of
the pastoral council is to see that stewardship happens. Your first
decision, then, will probably be to decide what kind of stewardship

leadership model will work best for your parish. Where will you place it? Check out "The Big Questions" below. Once you've made that decision, move on to the following steps. They are not in any order, but they all need to be addressed.

■ Never Deviate from Your One Message

When a parish commits to a focus on opportunities for faith growth and a new understanding of stewardship, the mission and the goal of parish life are set. Those goals are so all-inclusive that they will dominate parish life. And that's OK. From the viewpoint of the person in the pew, however, a seismic shift might have just taken place. Most older Catholics grew up in parishes that offered a warm, fuzzy Catholic ghetto with lots of familiar ritual like novenas and benedictions, comfortable rote responses like rosaries and litanies, and an inward-focused social life like gambling trips to nearby Native American casinos. If their children attended the parish school, then an additional layer of activity was added to the mix. Think Scout troops and candy sales. Catholic boys married Catholic girls. There were no homosexual Catholics. There were no divorced Catholics.

Now, Father is talking about a new kind of church. He is describing a new way of being Catholic that doesn't fit the old mold. While the challenge of change in any organization has many facets, the particular focus here is that of consistency of message. The most obvious disconnect, already described, is that of using the term "stewardship" simply as a catch phrase for giving more money. But the big picture is, in fact, much bigger. According to the studies done in the church, many disenchanted parishioners have already left—forty percent are "actively disengaged" and may never be seen in church again. The numbers are clear, and probably most would acknowledge this. But the parish still includes many others on the cusp, as it were—thirty percent are "inactive"—only seen perhaps at Christmas or Easter, the ones still on the mailing list but who are essentially invisible. And even among the thirty percent counted as "involved," we know that they can still be subdivided in to "parishioners" and "Mass-goers."

Change will begin to happen, initially at least for those who are active and involved. To become sustained and go beyond that group, however, the message of change must be unswerving, where each proclamation of it contains a harmony of meaning. This must happen both in the spoken message and from the message lived out in the lives of its members, both in what we say and what we do. Each of these parts of the message has its own challenges.

The proclamation of the message will come first and foremost from the priests and deacons in their homilies. All priests and deacons are responsible for their own homilies, and no pastor would want to remove that prerogative from them. But when a parish is making a major shift in such fundamental areas as a pro-active, multifaceted faith development and a redefinition of terms like stewardship, two options emerge. First, the pastor can give all homilies on certain Sundays so as to guarantee consistency of theme and content from Mass to Mass. Second, the pastor, the deacon, and any parochial vicars can work together in the preparation of their Sunday homilies at their monthly meetings where pastoral decisions are addressed, so that all homilies give the same message.

Not every priest or deacon may be happy with the second idea. But while nothing presented here is so radical that a priest could have difficulty preaching on it, the parish needs a consistent, enthusiastic response that is not set aside in favor of a different homiletic message. However accomplished, the spoken message must be the same from everyone and must be repeated many times to have any long-lasting impact.

The importance of integrity of the lived-out message is equally true. Evangelization needs to begin with parish leadership—the staff, the pastoral council, all ministry leaders—everyone involved in the life of the church. It needs to happen with catechists as well as coaches, with music leaders and Scout troop leaders, with the sacristan, the custodian, the plant manager, the teachers in the school, the yard aides, the rectory cook, the high school student receptionists—with everyone. If the parish is to have an authentic life of prayer, then every organization and club needs to support that goal, since these groups are major sources of contact for many parishioners. Group and club leaders need to be a focus of evangelization so they can do so authentically.

This work of faith development is no small task.

■ Work for Excellence

Do you want your members to be proud of their parish? The answer should be obvious. Then never accept "average." The next time you drive up to your parish, put on fresh eyes and look at it from the point of view of someone not very connected to the place. Go back to the questions in Chapter 1 about the appearance of the grounds. Review the questions found later in Chapter 9 about the attitude of everyone you meet there. What does it look like? How do you feel about being there? How warmly were you welcomed? However superficial they are, first impressions still mean a lot to most people, and obviously to strangers. You never get a second chance to make a first impression. What must be done to make the parish a place of pride for all who belong there? But then, go beyond the external.

A servant leader never blames others. Instead, always ask, over and over, "What can we do to make the parish more inviting and accepting?" If we place the blame for non-involvement on those not involved, nothing will ever change. The non-involved will stay so.

In most Catholic parishes, as was noted before, thirty percent of the families are involved, thirty percent are uninvolved, and forty percent are actively disengaged. In real terms, out of 1,000 families registered and in the parish database, only 300 are present for parish activities. Another 300 are still on the mailing list but don't participate in anything—maybe Mass on Christmas. And 400 would probably want to be removed from the mailing list if asked.

In the broader community, not just churches, conventional wisdom suggests that in most organizations, eighty percent of the work gets done by twenty percent of the people. However cynical, the 80-20 rule seems to make sense.

None of these numbers is encouraging, but they should come as no surprise to anyone in parish leadership. Your parish's experience might be slightly better or slightly worse than these findings suggest, but the reality is still true. We must face the fact that what we are doing and have been doing for a long time just doesn't work very well. The evidence suggests just as strongly that what does work is to make the church encounter more personal and more authentically prayerful. We must take the many steps necessary to encourage genuine involvement in the life of the parish; we must provide countless different opportunities for faith development, especially through peer ministry, always helping members to move from evangelization to catechesis to ministry (see Chapter 3); and all these steps must take precedence over fundraising.

This work has no finish line or time limit. Don't look for some kind of benchmark that tells you you're finished. It must become the ongoing work of the church—building up the body of Christ.

■ Begin an Annual Pledge of the Three Ts

Now is the time to genuinely move stewardship away from homilies about donating more money. Consider this scenario from my favorite mythical parish, St. Brunhilde's in East Overshoe, New Jersey.

Starting on the first Sunday after Christmas, Father spoke at all the Masses for three consecutive weeks on the broadened definition of stewardship, asking everyone to recall the great sense of thanks that everyone had just experienced during the holidays and translating the response to the gifts they had received into parish terms. He also announced that the annual donation letters for tax use would not be mailed until the end of the month, creating a slight murmur across the assembly. Instead, he told his flock, the letters would be given out in person at an important Town Hall meeting to be held on January 25. He made a strong appeal for everyone to attend. After all, he said, these meetings didn't happen very often. He added that refreshments would be served and that child care would be provided—no babysitters would be needed.

Later, after Mass, he began a lengthy process of personal invitations, starting with all those he met on the steps of the church, and continuing with visits to the school Parent-Teacher Guild and many different parish organizations at their January meetings. On every possible occasion, he not only made a presentation to the group but privately approached individual families to ask them to attend the January 25 meeting. During the informal chatter following Father's visits, everyone commented on the importance that he seemed to place on this meeting and the invitation that he had personally extended to each of them.

Throughout the month, bulletin articles and pulpit announcements continued to bolster his message. The parish receptionists gave flyers in the form of invitations to all visitors when they came into the office. These invitations also went home to each school family in the weekly information packet. He had already spent several meetings bringing staff, faculty, and pastoral council members on board, so that they, too, could share in inviting many different families to come together with the rest of the parish.

January 25 finally arrived. The parish hall was sparkling clean, brightly lit, and nicely decorated. Plenty of chairs were arranged for everyone's comfort. The P.A. system had been checked in advance and was properly tuned. Older parishioners, or those with hearing difficulties, were escorted by greeters to special seats at the front of the assembly. Fresh coffee (regular and decaf), tea, and delicious coffee cake prepared by the Ladies' Guild were available. Child care directed by responsible adults and teen club members was available in an adjoining room for families with small children. Father and his ministry leadership team had also developed the format of the presentation ahead of time so that all knew their parts.

The meeting began promptly. After all, honoring the time commitment of everyone there was a sign of respect for them. Handouts for the opening and closing prayers had been placed on all chairs ahead of time. Father had asked and prepared a team of lay ministry leaders to lead those prayers so that parishioners would see that priests are not the only ones who do that. After the prayer, Father began the meeting by expressing genuine thanks to everyone for investing their valuable time in an important parish meeting. Then, he and certain key leaders began the program, which included a well-developed PowerPoint presentation. Of course, PowerPoint printouts that included note space for each slide were also distributed. He had made certain that many of the slides included photos of parish events and lots of familiar faces. Everyone cheered when they saw their own!

At the heart of his message was the plan to look for two things from everyone there. First, he asked that each family expand its thinking of what it means to contribute to the parish. He spoke of the flaw in the many presentations that had been given on the subject of stewardship over the years, of how it was always really a code word for giving more money, of how the parish was moving to a broader recognition of time and talent, as well as treasure—and beginning to treat each of them equally. He acknowledged the difficult economic times and the reality that many families might be "light" on the treasure part at the moment. He then asked each family to think about making a pledge of time and talent to the church for the coming year. He acknowledged that this was a new idea for many parishioners, who might require some time to think about it.

Then, he swallowed hard and moved into new territory. He asked each family to consider making a similar pledge of treasure for the year. He acknowledged that such a step was not common in Catholic parishes and that most everyone might be familiar with it only from the recent capital campaign. But, he explained, this would be very helpful as the parish began to formulate its new budget.

Each family then received a personalized packet that included six parts, which he explained:

- First, the many opportunities to make a gift of time through service to the parish were listed in a large booklet: catechetical ministries, liturgical ministries, school ministries, office assistance, the sports program, and on and on. Not only was the booklet attractively designed and crafted, it was very thorough, with well-written "job descriptions" of every imaginable ministerial opportunity available across parish life. These articles included descriptions of the ministry, the skills required, the name and telephone number of a key contact or ministry leader, and, most important, the length of the term of service that was being asked for.

- Second, the parish was asking for all members to describe their gifts, their talents, their occupational skills, and their hobbies. All of these gifts would be added to the family database. He explained that a time might come when a person would be called upon for their particular gift.

- Third, a pledge of treasure for the coming year was included. The pledge form made clear that, just like the capital campaign, this was a moral promise and not a legal one.

- Fourth, all existing opportunities for faith growth and prayer were described along with ways to become involved in them. The description went further, however. It also asked for suggestions of additional offerings that might better meet individual needs.

- Fifth, a printout of everything known about the family from the parish database was included. It had been intentionally constructed so as to include opportunities to fill in missing parts: e-mail addresses, names and dates of birth of all family members, similar information on any other family adults living in the household, like grandparents, Sacramental history, helpful alumni information, like years of graduation or names and addresses of adult children who had graduated from the parish school. Everyone was asked to proofread this listing and bring the parish up to date with corrections and additions.

- Oh yes, the sixth item in the envelope was the family's annual donation letter. Each had been hand-signed and annotated by the pastor.

Everyone was given the opportunity to ask questions or to offer feedback about this surprising new approach. Father and others on the ministry leadership team answered each question, always respecting and thanking the person who had asked it. The entire team stressed the voluntary nature of this and that it was entirely OK if someone declined to participate. He did ask that anyone so declining would share the reason with him confidentially.

Father then invited each family to talk privately among themselves and complete the appropriate pages. Each packet included enough individual sheets to accommodate all members of the family, and ministry leaders had been prepped with additional copies for anyone who needed more. Families were also asked to share any strong feelings about this new plan, whether they be positive or negative. Envelopes were also enclosed so that privacy was assured. While each family was strongly encouraged to complete its pledge at the meeting, Father assured them it was OK to bring it to the parish office later that week. But human nature being what it is, he gave them enough time to complete their pledges on the spot if at all possible.

Parishioners had been promised that the meeting would last no more than one hour, and the team was determined to be faithful to that. After an appropriate amount of time, everyone was asked to bring their pledges forward and put them in a large basket placed prominently for that purpose. The closing prayer centered on the rich offerings of time, talent, and treasure that were made by members of the body of Christ and placed in that basket. Children in the adjoining child care room were invited to rejoin their families, and everyone shared in additional refreshments and fellowship after prayer.

In the days following, the leadership team thoroughly evaluated all responses. The most important point, Father stressed, was that everyone knew that this information was being acted upon and used and that the meeting had not been an exercise in futility. He asked each ministry leader to telephone a share of all respondents personally to express thanks and to invite them into ministries, based upon their response. They also telephoned each family that had not yet returned their completed forms to the parish. Father himself called anyone who had expressed a strong personal opinion about this new approach to giving.

In the weeks and months following, Father included in one homily each month a reflection on one additional aspect of stewardship. These topics were bolstered with bulletin inserts and Web site articles. He spoke of stewardship of *prayer*, encouraging members to strengthen their relationships with Jesus and providing guides to different prayer approaches consistent with lay life demands; stewardship of *money*, asking to take positive steps to live within their means and place the Lord first in their giving; stewardship of personal *health*, resolving to get more frequent check-ups and to use healthier eating habits, shunning fast foods, getting more exercise and the like. Over a period of a year, he also added stewardship of *work, the poor, neighborhoods, and family.*

With these steps, St. Brunhilde Church turned the page and began a new life of stewardship.

Your parish can do the same.

▪ Does the Pastor Like Coffee?

Back in my diocesan days, I tried to reach each parish. This was a daunting challenge since I had two hundred parishes to try to cover in the Albany, New York diocese. In my time management book—this was way before BlackBerries, or even DayTimers—I would faithfully write down three to five parishes for each week. My goal was to try to call one parish each day—that seemed workable. After all, these calls had no real agenda, just an informal opportunity to check in with a pastor or youth minister, to say "Hello," to find out if we could be of assistance in any way. It always seemed like an achievable goal. But busyness and procrastination would frequently get in the way. I would skip one because the pastor was grumpy or the youth minister would never return a call or I just didn't have time that day, or whatever. It was very difficult to sustain.

Later, I set as a goal to spend one month each summer visiting one county of the Albany diocese at a time. I sent out letters in advance and then telephoned each pastor to make sure vacation plans wouldn't be in the way. Then I would head out into the boondocks. Albany had many, many very rural parishes. In one case, in a small town parish that shall remain nameless, I knocked at the front door. Father answered. (No housekeeper here—the parish was too small for that.) He was a Polish priest who had come to the United States as a Displaced Person following World War II. He was astounded to be visited by a diocesan representative. In his several years as a pastor, he told me, no one from a diocesan office had ever come to visit him! And, I had managed to correctly pronounce his multi-syllabic Polish name. "Come in," he exclaimed with a jovial invitation, "Have a beer with me." It was a warm July afternoon. One beer led to two, which was a mistake—I still had a seventy-five-mile drive back to Albany. He explained that his parish was too small and the congregation was too old to have a youth program, but in the end, his enthusiasm was so great that he became a tremendous advocate for youth ministry with other priests at deanery meetings. We became good friends, and this particular personal encounter had a great payoff.

It isn't easy to develop the personal discipline to make this happen, but every time I did it the reward was apparent and would remind me of why it was so important to do it. The summers spent in parishes in the Catskills and the Adirondacks were particularly fruitful (and enjoyable). It should be the same for the pastor. In an era of shrinking priest numbers, however, perhaps one connection each day is too ambitious. Then aim for one each week. Just spend an hour each week with one parishioner at a time—perhaps a lay catechetical minister, perhaps a teacher in the school, or a pastoral council member, or the head of the ushers, or the person seen every morning at the 6:30 Mass, or a parishioner-business owner. It might be over a cup of coffee, or breakfast in the rectory, or a bag lunch in the park. But imagine the impact of these encounters when each person realized that Father just gave an hour of his time to be with them. Fifty key parishioners each year might be prompted to become more involved in the life of the parish. Is your parish still fortunate enough to have two priests? What if the parochial vicar took on the same goal? One hundred people might be persuaded to enter into deeper relationships with Jesus Christ and with the parish.

By the way, always have decaf after noon. And, avoid a second beer on warm July afternoons.

■ Does the Pastor Like People?

We certainly hope that he does! We hope that he places reaching out to everyone at the very center of his ministry. We hope that he offers many different entry points for others to become involved. We hope that his humanness and his message together open the door of welcome to everyone in and around the parish. We also hope that he first invites others who like people to join with him as ministry leaders in this endless process of being church.

Relational ministry is at the very heart of the faith development process—this can't be stated often enough. Evangelization, the first step, begins when one person sees faith modeled in the life of another and accepts the invitation to walk the walk together. It will never happen with homilies or pulpit messages or announcements by the president of the Parent-Teacher Guild alone. It happens only when all those people reach out in person.

Of course, we hope that the pastor likes people—even more than he likes coffee (or beer).

■ Repeat the Message—Over and Over!

In Chapter 15 I'll define two words from the world of advertising: "reach" and "frequency." Simply put, "reach" means how many different members get the message and "frequency" describes the number of times your communications reach any one member. Frequency seems to be more important, and most advertising specialists understand that in today's media-overloaded world it is necessary to repeat the message at least *three times* to each hearer for it to *begin* to be effective. With that thought in mind, it makes sense why advertisers repeat TV commercials over and over again.

This concept has tremendous ramifications for parishes. If a new movement is taking place in the parish, one that essentially redefines stewardship, or at least the way that word is understood by many church members, or one that places a whole new emphasis on faith development or on welcoming, then one announcement from the pulpit heralding this brave new world won't be enough. The pastor and other ministry leaders must understand that it will need to be repeated and repeated and repeated. Stewardship can't be preached only on "Stewardship Sunday." It must be a constant theme because it is at the heart of parish life and what it means to be Catholic.

Of course, the first group of parishioners who will need to hear it will be the ministry leaders themselves. By evangelizing the staff, the pastoral council, the school faculty, and all the many leaders of individual ministries, change will begin to be understood. By talking about these new ways over and over at staff, council, organization, and board meetings, it will finally begin to take hold. When the leadership team is all speaking with the same voice, then the message stands a better chance of reaching the person in the pew.

■ Can We Become a Paperless Parish?

Probably not. Every parish will always need to mail out annual donation-total letters, although at least one parish took the suggestion described earlier. The letters were given out in person, along with offertory envelopes for the new year, at a Town Hall meeting where each family was encouraged to make an annual pledge not only of treasure but of time and talent as well. Parishes will certainly always distribute Sunday bulletins, although some parishes also e-mail them each week. They will always use newsletters and e-mails and flyers and other mailings to announce upcoming events. It's difficult to see a paperless parish.

But the point here is not just to move from paper to e-mail, although that is important to do. The point is to begin to move away from paper communications—bulletins and flyers and mailings and letters—and move more toward *personal encounters* when you are inviting others to join in your mission. The moment of invitation must be person to person. The invitation to one hundred families each year to become more a part of the life of the church suggested a few paragraphs back won't happen by paper letters.

■ Invite, Invite, Invite

Over and over, always remember that Jesus didn't wait for volunteers, he invited others to share in his ministry. Ministers, not volunteers—the mantra of the new Catholic parish. Use every opportunity for people contact to invite others to join in. Invite those you know who might need a gentle nudge to go more deeply. Invite others who are new to you to become friends. A servant leader doesn't blame the others for their non-involvement but reaches out instead on every occasion to invite them in.

Every gathering that takes place—chats on the steps of the church after Mass, someone coming into the office to pick up a calendar, organization meetings, Town Hall meetings, parents coming to pick up their children after Saturday morning religious education classes—each is an occasion for invitation, an occasion for ministry. Invitations to have a cup of coffee, to share in a neighborhood potluck dinner, to complete a survey about satisfaction with parish life, or to put to use a talent on behalf of the parish—it makes no difference. Each ministry leader must put invitation at the top of their "To Do" list—invitation to join in the mission of the parish. (Invitation is a major component described in much more detail in Chapter 7.)

■ Your Own Road Map

If you need to drive from New York to Los Angeles, there are two ways to look for road maps. One is to do a Google map search on those two points. The results will give you a step-by-step plan: "Start here, go X miles on route A to B, then turn right and go X more miles on route C to D, and on and on." The directions will be very precise. Map blow-ups of intersections will be included. Sometimes you will even see photos of important points along the way. Sort of a computerized version of the old AAA "Trip-Tik." That's one way. There is no Google counterpart for the pathway to stewardship.

The other way to reach Los Angeles is to take a paper map and look at where you are and where you want to be. You can use your yellow highlighter to mark out many different routes. Hopefully, they will all get you there. Some might be more direct than others. Some will have interesting side adventures.

Your road map to becoming a great (or stewardship) parish will be like that. Don't expect a Google printout to show you how to get from Here to There. Your map won't be like anyone else's. You have to figure it out for yourself. The Good News is that you will have the guidance of the Holy Spirit in laying out your path. Getting from Here to There is what this book is all about.

THE BIG QUESTIONS

Given that stewardship is not a program but an underlying pastoral theology, how does your parish approach the question of a "lead agent" for stewardship. First, examine all your leadership structures as they now exist. Is the pastoral council equipped or able to take it on? Do they have the time? Is their plate already full with temporal affairs? Do they have the people to do it? If they cannot do it, do you have another ministry committee whose work is already close enough to stewardship that they could easily add this to their agenda? Or, do you look to create an entirely new committee? How is it constituted? Is it made up of representatives from each of the many different areas of parish life? Or is it a new body with new people? Will it work alongside other committees? Or will it have a supervisory role, perhaps as an adjunct of the pastoral council? Regardless of its formation and composition, what kind of faith formation and training will they need? Which staff member will be responsible for their guidance and growth?

BIBLIOGRAPHY AND ASSOCIATED RESOURCES

The Prayer for Stewardship found at the beginning of this chapter came from the Stewardship Office of the Diocese of Colorado Springs, Colorado. You can find it on their Web site at www.diocs.org/Stewardship/prayers.cfm.

The U.S. Catholic bishops offered a pastoral letter titled *Stewardship: A Disciple's Response* that provided a foundational definition of stewardship in the best possible terms. Copies may be purchased from www.usccbpublishing.org.

The International Catholic Stewardship Council is an excellent (if somewhat expensive) resource to help broaden the definition of stewardship. Their annual conferences are excellent! You can find them at:

> International Catholic Stewardship Council
> 1275 K Street NW, Suite 880
> Washington, DC 20005-4006
> Tel: 2022891093. Fax: 2026829018
> E-mail: icsc@catholicstewardship.org
> Web site: www.catholicstewardship.org

Many dioceses, or course, have stewardship offices. One particularly good one is the Diocese of Rockville Centre (Long Island). Go to www.stewardshipli.org to get on their mailing list. If you live in the Northeast, their conferences are also very good.

Warning: A Google search on "stewardship" will produce hundreds of references to fundraising consultants.

CHAPTER 6

Must We Talk about Money Again?
Financial Giving

> Each of you must give as you have made up your mind, not reluctantly or under compulsion, *for God loves a cheerful giver*.
>
> 2 Corinthians 9:7

M ust we talk about money again? Sometimes, the answer is "Yes." If we as ministry leaders of the parish are to be good stewards of the resources of the parish, included in that responsibility is effective and prudent management of the monetary part of those resources. We know what that means in plain and simple terms. At the minimum, we need enough money to pay the bills. Realistically, we must go beyond paying the bills and provide for the future.

It is clear both from the stewardship and development work of others and the experiences of great parishes and ordinary parishes as well that **people will give what they think the parish is worth**. All the other work that you do here on community building and inviting, affirming and evangelizing, catechizing and communicating, and sharing and praying together will help to create a great parish—when done authentically, intensively, and regularly. And when parish members know that their parish is great, they will be open to reflections on time, talent, and treasure. They will be open to saying "thank you" for all that they have. When they know that money is not the only subject from the pulpit, they will be less resistant or cynical on the occasions when it is the pulpit topic. When they hear a discussion about money as part of a larger one on different elements of stewardship, they won't see it as "secular" or dirty—something that has no place in church.

How do we handle requests for money? Do we have a very predictable approach?

1. Envelope sets are distributed to all parishioners, or at least those requesting them. It seems like a tragic paradox that some could ask to be considered members of a parish, yet decline to receive offering envelopes. Sadly, this is true in many parishes and may be a real indictment of what they are offered by the parish, how they feel about it, and how well they understand the Christian responsibilities of stewardship. But that is a subject covered in the broader discussion of the topic.

2. Every Sunday, a first collection (offertory) is taken and often a second may be as well (for the parish school, or the bishop's appeal, or for one of the many special appeals from the diocese).

3. Special second collections are taken from time to time when a visiting missionary appears or for an important unforeseen purpose, like an earthquake in Haiti, a hurricane in New Orleans or a tsunami in Indonesia.

4. An extraordinary parish budgetary crisis might warrant an emergency request.

5. Occasional homilies are given on "stewardship," once again reducing its meaning to giving money. Most congregants tune the message out and later grumble to spouses about how the church is always asking for money.

6. Annual form letters summarizing donations are sent to all parishioners.

Everyone knows the drill. They know what's coming. **But, to paraphrase Albert Einstein's famous quotation about the definition of insanity, how do we hope for any different results if we keep doing the same thing over and over again?** If members support the parish enthusiastically and plentifully using this method, then perhaps no change is necessary. This is not the case for most parishes, however. Especially in difficult economic times, most are having trouble figuring out how to pay all the bills. We need to look for a better way.

The most important steps were covered in the previous chapter, where monetary giving is clearly shown to be only one part of the broader definition of stewardship. Hoping and presuming that you will have accepted and integrated those premises into your pastoral approach, we still need to deal specifically with those moments where it is necessary to ask for money.

Money should never be the first thing asked for, it should be the last. When it is the question, though, what are important issues? Trade places and think like the parishioner.

- Am I being asked to increase my offertory support (an ongoing gift to cover regular operating expenses) or am I being asked for a special gift to cover a unique cash outlay (a one-time gift or a pledge for a fixed term, like a capital campaign)?

- Is this a regular annual appeal, or is this an emergency? If an emergency, why?

- Is this an emergency to balance the budget or pay the bills? If so, have they told me what they will do next month, or next year? Will they be asking again for the next emergency?

- **Is the parish leadership absolutely transparent?** Have they told me what my donation will be used for? How will it help improve the parish community? Or is it needed for survival?

- Do we get regular reports from the leadership about the parish finances? Does the Sunday bulletin give me a regular report of weekly giving? Do I know how that compared to the weekly expense needs?

- Why are they asking me? Am I simply a name on their mailing list? Do I ever hear from them when they aren't asking for money? Do they want my involvement or do just want my money? In other words, is there a place for my time and my talent—my ministry—or just my check?

- **Who are the "they" in these questions? Do I feel a sense of ownership of the parish? (Is it "my" parish?) Do I feel like I belong there?**

- Do I have confidence in the parish leadership, both ordained and lay?

- Do they give me a feeling of confidence that the parish is in a good place, that they are strong, or does it feel that the ship is sinking?

- Does the parish have a long view, or does it simply seem to get by from year to year? Is there any strategic or long-range planning that I as a parishioner know about?

- Do I know what the overall mission or vision of the parish is?

- Did they acknowledge my last gift? Did they say "thank you" for it? Have they ever said "thank you"?

Behind so many of these questions is the disconnect between those doing the asking and those being asked. Mailing pieces won't do it. Neither will bulletin announcements or homilies about the grim budget realities of the parish. After all, if each Sunday bulletin contains a little box listing last week's offertory total and the amount needed each week to balance the budget, and if those numbers show a deficit each week, and if nothing seems to change in the parish, then no one will pay any attention to it, since it is apparently just a fluke of numbers. After all, "the church is rich."

Two things must change for this situation to get any better. The leadership of the parish must begin the slow, steady movement toward authentic people connections. And, they must ask why requests for giving have only to do with money. If stewardship means sharing one's time, talent and treasure, then it makes sense that appeals should be for all three equally—especially in difficult economic times.

For an agenda for change, use this simple approach. Go back to the list of questions just above and turn them into statements—your agenda for change.

- We will be absolutely transparent about our financial condition with members of the parish at all times. We will provide them with accurate financial reports quarterly. We will conduct an annual parish meeting where a budget for the next year will be presented. We will always tell parishioners what each collection is to be used for.

- We will give regular reports of weekly giving in each Sunday bulletin, along with the weekly operating cost. If the parish is operating at a deficit, we will explain what source of funds will be used to cover the loss, or how expenses will be reduced to eliminate the deficit.

- Our parish leadership will rethink the whole meaning of stewardship and place time and talent on equal footing with treasure. We will do this by valuing the ministry potential of each member of the parish.

- Through our transparency and a new sense of shared ministry, we will look to the time when each member can speak of "my" parish.

- We will work toward reaching a level of strength, both financial and moral, where members will have the confidence that the parish is in a good place.

- Our parish leadership will begin to take the long view by engaging in a process of strategic planning, even if that means seeking assistance from professionals with the skills to lead us through it. And we will make parishioners a part of this process so they share in the ownership of it.

- Our parish leadership will regularly communicate the mission or vision of the parish to all the members.

- We will acknowledge every gift. We will always say "thank you," whatever the size of the gift. We will constantly thank the parishioners for their generosity.

- The most challenging change of all is for the parish itself to tithe. That is, the parish pledges to give a declared percentage (ten percent??) of its revenue to others in need. While this step might seem to make no sense if the parish is itself struggling, have faith that if the parish tithes, some parishioners will also tithe.

These might sound like pie-in-the-sky New Year's resolutions, but then perhaps the parish needs lofty goals to aim for. It might be a time for big dreams. After all, the changes that are needed look to a fundamental redefinition of being Catholic and belonging to a parish—new approaches toward faith development, new approaches toward stewardship. Once again, a discussion about giving money becomes part of a much larger one about changing everything.

First, look at all the suggestions for "in-reach," meaning what we do to connect with those within the parish, in Chapter 14. Every step described in that chapter is about real, one-on-one people contact. It is that kind of relationship-building that will lead to real change in parish life, not just around giving money, but with the attitude of church members toward the parish as a whole. A closely related task is the need to take a hard look at the way it communicates with members on the grand scale. Chapter 15 describes many different ways to reach everyone when one-on-one is not possible. A key question in both these chapters is "How often and in what ways do we communicate with our inactive members?"

Moving from just asking for money to equal requests for gifts of time, of talent, and of treasure is the other big change. This is at the heart of the new model of stewardship. It may be necessary for your parish to postpone its decision to begin a capital campaign, for instance, if it is clear that you haven't reached this point of understanding stewardship. Don't set yourself up for failure. Don't get taken in by slick proposals from fundraising consultants who claim that they have a surefire way to raise money.

Yes, it is true that these ideas seem to repeat those described in the previous chapter, where the topic was *not* about giving money. Of course, that's because the issues are exactly the same. People's relationship to the parish and how and what they will decide to give will both change when relational ministry and faith development take place.

■ Are You Ready for Electronic Giving?

What next? If you've done a collective examination of conscience and believe that you must ask for money when necessity dictates it, one relatively new method of giving seems to have been overlooked: electronic giving. Catholic parishes have been slow to move in this direction, although many Protestant churches have used it for several years. Catholic schools have a much longer tradition for payment of tuition and fees.

What Is It? How Does It Work?

Just as many are now comfortable using an automatic bank withdrawal system to pay regular bills, like utilities or credit cards, churches can use similar systems to regularly withdraw agreed amounts from parishioners' bank accounts for offerings. Your bank may have facilities to do this for you, but third-party computer programs designed specifically for church use are also available.

Two methods of electronic giving are the most popular, ACH or bank draft giving (the same) and credit card giving. Kiosk giving is now a third option added to the mix.

- ACH or bank draft giving is most popular because it is cheaper than credit cards and it withdraws funds that members already have in the bank. In ACH giving, the member completes and signs an agreement with the church that specifies a regular weekly donation amount, the frequency of withdrawals (usually monthly or twice monthly), how to handle months with five Sundays instead of four, and their bank account information (usually the numbers found on the bottom of the check). This agreement form should be available on the parish Web site. This information is entered into computer software provided by the bank or third-party vendor used for this purpose, and the transaction occurs on a prescribed date each month when the software is activated and the data sent via the Internet to the bank. Reports provided by the software package provide a complete listing of individual donations, which can be recorded just like any cash bank deposit. Information about refused transactions, or "bounces," comes back to you in a few days, usually via e-mail.

- Banks increasingly offer the opportunity for churches to provide a donation kiosk right on church property, perhaps in the parish office, perhaps in the church vestibule. `This option is still distasteful to many church members.

- Credit card giving is also available but is slightly less popular. Well-meaning members might commit to donations based on credit that are larger than they can handle, thus creating credit card debt that they will find difficult to repay and come to regret. Some pastors may feel that this way of giving runs contrary to what churches should teach regarding financial responsibility. Additionally, transaction fees charged by the bank are higher for credit cards than bank draft. Nevertheless, some churches find it useful to have credit card transaction ability and a "swipe" machine in the parish office for occasional or special donor use. Parishioners will also appreciate this option for purchasing tickets to fundraising dinners or other parish events, for paying fees for parish educational programs, and the like. Some members will use it exclusively to generate miles in their card accounts.

■ The Pros

Electronic giving smooths out cash flow. By far, this is the most popular value that parishes see with electronic giving. You know that on the fifth of each month, for instance, a predictable amount of donations will be received. (Bank statistics usually suggest the fifth and twentieth of each month are the best days for ACH transactions.)

Donations generally increase with electronic giving, for reasons not entirely understood. One large parish near Washington, DC, found that those using electronic giving donated sixteen percent more per family than those using envelopes. Another broader recent study of non-profit organizations found than online donors gave as much as fifty percent more than those using traditional means.

Overall donation totals also show an increase, since members have a way of giving regularly whether they are at Mass or not. They do not fluctuate as much during vacation time or during flu season or when the weather is bad or when a particularly important NFL game is played early.

Electronic giving can be especially helpful if your parish has a significant "snow bunny" population that spends winters at a different location.

It becomes automatic, and many busy people who genuinely want to give to their church will be grateful to have the task removed from their "to do" list.

It's like a payroll deduction. It happens automatically. It comes off the top. It becomes easier to live without it when we never saw it to begin with.

Many people no longer carry their checkbook with them.

For infirm members or former parishioners who live miles away but still have warm feelings for the parish, electronic giving may be the only practical way to contribute.

Catholic schools will find electronic giving particularly valuable for alumni donations.

This method of giving seems to be more acceptable as online bill payment becomes the way that we handle our overall cash outlays each month. Most parishes using electronic giving find that a few more people start using it each time they promote it. One parish reported a great response by including an enrollment with its annual January donation "thank you" letter.

Transaction details can be changed, suspended, or canceled at any time by the donor with a telephone call or e-mail.

More people become computer-savvy all the time, resulting in a higher trust level and less suspicion about electronic giving.

It is offered as one way, not the only way, to make donations to the church.

Some might choose electronic giving for specific purposes, like a capital campaign, while still using envelopes each week for their regular contributions.

Electronic giving can reduce the burden on the weekly Collection Committee, since less cash and fewer checks come to the church via the collection basket. It can potentially also reduce the amount of courier-handled bank deposits.

Bank service charges (typically higher on business accounts like the ones used by most churches) generally go down because fewer checks pass though the system. Banks like ACH transactions, because they reduce the amount of paper being handled.

■ The Cons

Electronic giving, because it is handled invisibly, removes the need to make a conscious decision each week to give to the church. The act of giving, which ought to be a prayerful moment, becomes automated. Since the decision to give is such an important one, this is no small matter.

Some parishioners will see this as yet a further depersonalization of the church. In one large parish, one member was adamantly opposed to electronic giving. She was convinced that a large number of the congregation would leave the church because of its introduction, even though it was offered as one option and no one would be required to use it.

By far, churches with younger congregations use electronic giving more and those with older congregations use it less.

Some will be uncomfortable with not placing an envelope in the collection basket and feeling the presumed scorn of their pew mates. Provisions need to be made to mitigate this. One church prints a line declaring "Electronic donor" on the donation envelopes with a check-off box. Another has envelope-sized, uniformly colored paper slips available for pickup in the vestibule that can be placed in the basket instead. ("I proudly donate to St. Brunhilde parish electronically!")

Handling donations for Easter and Christmas, for special parish appeals, and for the many second collections required by the diocese presents a special problem, since individual giving varies wildly according to specific member interests. Most parishioners want to give larger amounts for Easter and Christmas. In one parish, the Christmas collection was three times the amount of a typical Sunday. Special parish appeals and diocesan second collections present another challenge. Donations for Catholic University of America might be only a fraction of the amount taken for Catholic Relief Services. Your parish numbers will be different, but the challenge is the same. These donations must either still be made with envelopes, or provisions for member declarations of donation amounts need to be developed. One parish asks its printer to insert a line on the front of all second collection envelopes: "We give electronically. Please deduct $_____ on the next debit for this collection."

THE BIG QUESTIONS

If your parish's financial condition is not rock solid, what steps can you take both immediately and over the next two to three years to improve it? What plan for change do you have—in conjunction with those on the broader issue of stewardship in the last chapter—that move parishioners to a better understanding of gifts of time, talent, and treasure? Discuss the biblical imperative to tithe—as a parish. The openness to tithing will come only when significant, ongoing evangelization of parish ministerial leaders has taken place.

Electronic giving can be a "hot button" issue. Begin the discussion with the pastoral council, since it probably represents the broadest set of parishioners. Then, prepare a Sunday bulletin insert telling everyone that the parish is **considering** electronic giving, as one option to be added to the mix. Using points from earlier in this chapter, describe the process and some of the pros and cons. Ask how many would be interested. Ask also for opinions about the plan. Finally, go to the finance council and the pastor with the pastoral council's and parishioners' views for a decision.

BIBLIOGRAPHY AND ASSOCIATED RESOURCES

The Association of Fundraising Professionals (www.afpnet.org) can point you to many resources through its consultants directory. Their consultants and resource directory contains *paid* listings of consultants and organizations that provide products and services to the fundraising and nonprofit community.

If you are interested in electronic giving, begin with your own bank. Every bank offers ACH services. Then, do a Google search on "ACH services" for comparative information.

CHAPTER 7

Invite, Invite, Invite
Jesus Never Waited for Volunteers

And he said to them, "Follow me, and I will make you fish for people." Immediately they left their nets and followed him.

Matthew 4:19–20

Father Andrew Greeley once challenged us to consider the notion that perhaps we don't have a shortage of priests. Maybe what we have here is the Holy Spirit nudging us into facing the truth about what our role in the church was always supposed to be, a shared ministry between the clergy and the laity. In fact, a case can be made that the mission of the church becomes more realized when laypeople are its ministers, when laypeople evangelize. Priests do not live in the world of laypeople. The witness of one layperson to another is immensely powerful, in some ways more powerful than that of a priest.

During the early 1980s, the Youth Ministry Offices of the eight Northern California Dioceses (Fresno, Monterey, Oakland, San Francisco, San Jose, Sacramento, Santa Rosa, and Stockton) collectively conducted the Emmaus Program, where young (and some not so young) adults were trained and prepared to give a year of full-time service developing youth ministry in a parish. In addition to helping with the formation of a core group, working extensively with the pastor, and offering regular supervision and support all year, the board provided the participants with five weeks of training before they began their year.

We gathered each summer, for the eight years of the Emmaus program's existence. It became the custom on the opening day, in lieu of fancy ice-breakers, to hold an open-ended session where each participant could take as much time as was needed to tell his or her story. Essentially, they related what adventures had brought each of them from wherever they began to "right here, right now."

Those sessions were revealing, rich moments. After all, how often do we receive an invitation to be solely in the spotlight? No questions, no interruptions, no joining in were allowed. We were always struck by two patterns that emerged from this sharing each year.

Most of the participants told long, circuitous tales, often about rocky, faith-challenging times. I don't remember even one person ever speaking of awakening one day at the age of sixteen or eighteen saying, "I want to become a youth minister!" Most brought huge piles of life experiences with them, both inside and outside the Church, leading to this moment. This pattern existed for *most*. (As an aside, that reality alone contributed to the wide use of Malcolm Knowles' educational approach, called andragogy, as compared to pedagogy. I elaborate on this below.)

Another pattern existed for *all* of them. Each of them could inevitably point to a moment of invitation. Each person without fail told of a particular instant where someone invited them into ministry. As each year's program unfolded and this characteristic repeated itself, The Truth about ministry became very clear: *Jesus never waits for volunteers. Jesus always invites.* Scripture stories are full of such moments. Jesus personally invited each of the Twelve. And, through the words and actions of others, he invites all of us today. In our roles as ministerial leaders, one of our principal tasks is to invite others to share our ministries as well.

A Personal Story

My own moment of invitation began outside our parish church, St. Elizabeth's in Granite City, Illinois, after Mass on an October Sunday. I was leaving church with my parents, and we stopped to chat for a moment with our pastor, Fr. Lawrence Mattingly. He asked me if I would cover for the adult moderator of the teen club, who was going to be away for two weeks. After all, I had worked for five years during high school and college with kids at the local YMCA. "Two weeks; no problem," I thought, and agreed. Two weeks led to nine years with my parish and, later, a change in career direction that moved me into diocesan work in Albany, New York, for seven years, archdiocesan work in San Francisco for eleven years, and various parish management positions at the Church and School of the Epiphany in San Francisco (my present location) for more than sixteen years. My entire life's direction can be traced back to that one moment of invitation in 1962. I will bet you a cup of coffee that you can tell your own story of just such a moment.

No Volunteers Needed

Saint Peter writes that all of us, the whole people of God, are a chosen race, a royal priesthood, a people set apart, not only those who are ordained (1 Peter 2:9). This is the universal order of the faithful, the priesthood of the people that was unleashed by Pope John XXIII nearly fifty years ago. Now, we can see that it is the future of the church. Great parishes do not merely allow laypeople to do what was once the province of priests and sisters, they promote it and in fact count on it.

The job description, then, of ministry leaders—ordained, professed, and lay—must include a constant openness to everyone within the assembly to identify and invite members to share in and/ or lead individual ministries within the parish. This isn't always easy. Remembering back to the supervision of the Emmaus participants, for many, it was very difficult (and not as personally gratifying) to "let go" of working directly with young people and move into the role of supporting others to do that work.

This task—identifying, inviting, forming and training, and supporting—essentially means doing away with the term "volunteer." Because this model is built upon invitation, instead use the term "minister." Laypeople are just as certainly ministers as ordained priests and deacons are. That having been said, many of the concepts of volunteer management found in other publications still have value—they simply need to be translated into ministerial language—and they are incorporated into the four sections of this chapter: Identifying, Inviting, Forming and Training, and Supporting.

If we represented a service organization in the broader non-profit sector, we would speak of recruiting, interviewing, training, and mentoring volunteers. Because we are Catholic ministry leaders, we speak instead of identifying, inviting, forming and training, and supporting other ministers. We see our task as discerning that person's gifts from God—discerning, not recruiting; gifts, not skills. We help with the formation of ministers—working in a systematic way in another person's lifelong task of drawing closer to Jesus Christ. We speak of supporting another, as we walk the walk of faith together. While many of the underlying concepts from the world of volunteer management are still valid, we choose to use different vocabulary, partly because we approach the task differently and partially because our language tells everyone what we stand for, what we believe.

"All right," you say, "I'm a ministry leader. What exactly am I looking for in others?" Here are four steps to the process.

■ The Call to Ministry in Your Parish

Texas Instruments, a well-known electronics manufacturer, has a long and illustrious history of encouraging community service among its employees. It is famous for a landmark study that looked at what motivates people to serve others. The essence of its findings was that **most people choose to become volunteers for the same reason that they choose to work. The only difference is that they don't get paid, and** *that doesn't seem to make any difference*. Now, of course, serving as a minister is different from serving as a volunteer because of the added dimension of faith in God. Each of us responds to a call to ministry as part of an ongoing faith development. Millions of people everywhere choose to serve as volunteers for reasons having nothing to do with faith, which takes away nothing from the value of their service. Volunteering is a very American thing to do. One study suggests that more than fifty percent of the American population volunteers to do something each year, in all age groups, educational backgrounds, income levels, and sexes.

The ministry leader, then, can project many elements of management in the workplace into the management of ministers. The *management* of ministers means that giving a minister a positive experience of service to others, and getting good work from that minister, are management functions. And again, while much translating needs to be done, learning from the management of workers is a good place to start in the management of ministers.

One caution: Never invite others to serve, thinking that you're getting free labor. While it is true that there may be no outright compensation, there is a cost, including a time investment in screening, training, and scheduling, ongoing supervision and evaluation of ministers, recognition events like "Thank You" dinners and Christmas gifts, and, yes, the personal courage and energy it takes to occasionally dismiss or "fire" a minister.

▪ Identify Potential Ministries and Ministers

Potential Ministries

Begin by identifying potential ministry positions that need to be filled and creating job descriptions—specific, manageable, measurable, defined jobs; jobs with time limits on them, jobs with beginnings and ends, not open-ended; jobs with clearly defined responsibilities.

You are almost certain to have more success inviting someone to serve, for example, as a eucharistic minister at the 10 AM Mass for the school year than by asking, "Would you help out at Mass on Sundays?" Research indicates that potential ministers are more readily drawn to short-term commitments and those with more flexibility in scheduling, especially in a time of economic uncertainty. It is for leaders to tailor ministry opportunities to the needs and schedules of those who might serve.

Parishes with successful lay ministries frequently create a directory of ministry opportunities that reads very much like a group of job offerings. Each listing has a title of the position offered, the name of the parish program or ministry needing service, a one-paragraph description of the position, including particular skills required, and the duration of service needed for the ministry position. Here is a sample of the type of listing that might be found in a directory of ministry opportunities in the parish.

Ministry Opportunity: Bereavement Ministry, Grief Counselor. You will work as part of a team of other grief ministers who will make one-on-one contact with family members of recently deceased parishioners. You must be able to be "on call" and to respond to one-on-one needs as they arise; also able to participate in or lead annual Memorial Day and All Souls Prayer Services.

Training or Skills Required: Good listening skills. A high level of compassion and sense of empathy. Training is available through diocesan workshops. Lots of support is provided through prayer opportunities and other gatherings with your fellow grief ministers.

Length of Commitment: Two years.

Contact Info: Helen Canelo, Bereavement Ministry Coordinator. 415-123-4567.

Of course, most parishes are familiar with ministry fairs. The reason these events sometimes fail may have to do with lack of specificity. Simply having booths with brochures on the table but with no specific offerings probably won't lead to successful matches.

Potential Ministers

There will be parishioners who are very skillful in a particular area. There will be parishioners with deep faith. Oh, to find those who have both! But life is not always like that. Often, one encounters a parishioner whose faith life seems very rich and alive but who does not on the surface seem to have any particular leadership qualities. (Self-esteem does not always seem to move at the same speed as prayer life.) Or, one finds someone who is an absolute genius at solving a particular problem that the parish faces—like Web site management or roofing leaks—but who seems only lukewarm in matters of faith.

The task of the ministry leader is to take each person as is and, through discussions and explorations of different parish ministries, help move them to where they need to go. In the case of the prayerful parishioner, perhaps the task is to find an area the person might begin to explore, not as leader but as helper. It might take several attempts to find a good fit. The process for the genius problem-solver would be different. There, through affirmation, discussion, and invitation to prayer, the task might be to help the person see talents as gifts from God and getting the job done as ministry and response for those gifts. The ministry leader is called to do both, to accept each parishioner as a unique individual, and to help that person discern one's special direction in living out the call to ministry.

Ministry leaders should always be open to the special gifts and talents of everyone they meet across the spectrum of parish life. Listen to the conversation of fellow parishioners for indications that they are interested in some kind of service to the parish, even if they can't express it explicitly. Meetings with new parishioners should always include time for inquiries about their interests and talents. Always remember to include such findings in the parish database. Ministerial staff should learn to use the database program so that they can easily and effectively add ministry and gift information whenever it is discovered.

Let peer ministry work here. Periodically, invite dedicated parishioners to write articles for the Sunday bulletin or Web site offering reflections about being involved in different ministries. If they aren't writers, sit down at a keyboard and interview them. Take the lead in writing the article around their responses and then get their approval before publishing it. Be sure to include their picture if your bulletin easily handles graphics.

■ Invite

Understanding the many different motivations to serve can assist you in choosing whom to invite to serve, and how to do so. Volunteer motivation studies conducted over many years cite many different reasons, but they generally include a desire to help other people, an interest in the work of the organization, having free time, a desire to learn new skills or gain experience, seeking opportunities for personal achievement, knowing someone who already volunteers, devotion to a cause, and, of course, religious conviction.

If a parish has a fully integrated faith development model built upon relational ministry, then it becomes much easier to sort through these issues. After all, if you are walking the walk of faith with another person, from evangelization to catechesis to ministry, you will have had many opportunities through conversation and sharing and prayer to understand that person's motivation, and, most likely, the areas of potential ministerial interest.

Consequently, because someone says "No" once doesn't mean lack of interest. The person may be very busy, or be dealing with lots of personal issues. The particular request you are making may not be the right one.

In an era of increased sensitivity to past abuses and legal problems, if a candidate for potential ministry to children or youth emphatically declines such an invitation, it may well be appropriate simply to accept the answer or to ask the candidate if other areas of ministry are more appealing or appropriate. A related issue is the screening and fingerprinting required by every diocese in the United States. Look to your diocese for assistance with minister (volunteer) applications and criminal background screening and fingerprinting requirements. Yes, it is regrettable that such things are necessary, but proper protection of children and youth requires them. These steps are critical to the management of your ministry candidates.

■ Form and Train

Assistance with faith development and transmission of skills present two entirely different tasks.

Formation

Begin with formation, a *faith development undertaking*. Your first recognition as a ministry leader must be that you cannot *give* someone faith. Faith is a gift from God, not from you or me. You can (and should) model faith. You can provide prayerful opportunities for potential ministers to discover their faith. But it isn't yours to give.

The description of the faith development process covered in Chapter 3 applies equally to the formation of parish ministers, but here are some steps that seem most appropriate to this group.

Recognize that the task of helping others with their faith walk can take its toll. Even though an individual in this ministry might be comfortable with one's own faith walk, the questions that another person asks might trigger new ones for the minister. Make certain that "battery-charging" events *with other ministers in the same work* are offered frequently.

As the ministry director, keep yourself connected to the vast resources found on the Internet so that you can send helpful print pieces as e-mail attachments to your ministers—just to let them know that you are thinking about them.

Offer simple shared prayer opportunities for your ministers.

Recognize that your ministers are adults. Make certain that they receive resources for their own self-directed faith formation, like *Exploring the Sunday Readings*. (See Chapter 2.)

Training

This leads to the task of training potential ministers in their tasks— *an educational undertaking*. Most ministers will need training in human relations areas: teaching, facilitating, program plannin' leading, and the like. Since the ministry candidates needing to be trained will be adolescents, young adults, or adults, it is appropriate to consider an educational model best suited to them, andragogy. Whereas pedagogy, strictly defined, means the education of the child (From the Greek, *paid*, meaning child, and, *agogos*, meaning "to lead"), andragogy refers to the education of the adult (*andros*, meaning man, and *agogos*, meaning "to lead").

While the term "andragogy" was originally coined by a German educator in the 1830s, it only came into popular usage when it was adopted by the American educator Malcolm Knowles (*The Adult Learner: A Neglected Species*, 1973). Knowles promoted the concept of andragogy until his death in 1997. He proposed that adults have different learning needs from children, and accordingly require different educational models. Adults, Knowles contended, will learn best when certain conditions for learning are met. Compare the two models in the table shown on the next page.

TWO EDUCATIONAL MODELS		
ISSUE	PEDAGOGY	ANDRAGOGY
Built around five principles:		
The Learner's Self Concept	*The child learner has a dependent personality; the teacher directs what subjects are taught and how they are to be learned*	*Encouraged by the teacher, the adult learner moves toward independence and self-direction; needs to know why something needs to be learned; needs to be involved in the planning, construction, and evaluation of their instruction*
The Learner's Experience	*Has little or no experience to draw upon, relies mostly or entirely upon the teacher's direction or content; teaching methods are mostly didactic*	*Acquires a growing reservoir of experience (including past mistakes) that becomes an increasingly rich resource for learning*
The Learner's Readiness to Learn	*Children do not necessarily understand what they need to know; they are taught what society expects them to know, resulting in a standardized curriculum*	*Adults learn what they need to know; learning becomes increasingly oriented toward life application, or the subjects or skills that have immediate relevancy to role*
The Learner's Orientation to Learn	*Acquisition of subject matter; content-oriented; knowledge needed for later in life*	*Knowledge needed immediately, moves toward problem-solving*
The Learner's Motivation to Learn	*Need to learn is communicated by the teacher*	*Need to learn is motivated internally*

continued on page 112

continued from page 111

IMPORTANT POINT: *Knowles acknowledged that several of these assumptions apply in varying degrees both to adults and children. The differences are not etched in stone. Simply put, children tend to behave more often according to ways described in Column Two and adults tend to behave more often with the characteristics in Column Three. The operative words are "more often." Even Knowles acknowledged that some child learners operate in ways like adults and some adult learners operate in ways like children.*

Characteristics	*Passive reception*	*Active inquiry*
The role of the teacher	*Transmitter of information*	*Facilitator of learning*
What is taught	*The teacher's agenda*	*The learner's needs*
Relationship of teacher and student	*Education from above*	*Education of equals*
Approaches	*Transmission of information*	*Processes for learning, like discussion, problem-solving*
Designing educational models	*What content needs to be covered?* *How should this content be organized into modules?* *How can it be transmitted in logical sequence?* *What is the most effective method for transmitting that content?*	*How to design and manage a process for facilitating the acquisition of content by the learner* *How to serve as a content resource and provide connections to other content resources (peers, specialists, etc.)*

No study of the impact of the Internet upon the way children learn was done for this book, but the sense of inquiry that the Internet fosters may move some children, especially those of middle-school age or beyond, into realms of learning formerly thought appropriate by Knowles for adults.

Likewise, it is probably safe to presume that self-directed adults can address more learning needs personally through Internet inquiry than was once the case through books alone. Our own anecdotal evidence would support that notion.

The consequences of the andragogical model are very significant for the ministry leader. For some, making a shift from being a "teacher" to being a "facilitator of learning" may actually require a personal change of educational approach, if one's personal experiences have been entirely dominated by a pedagogical style of teaching. Andragogy uses personal learning contracts, learning teams, group sharing, mentors, and many other non-traditional techniques far removed from traditional classroom methodology.

■ Support

Some Volunteer Management Thoughts

In spite of the challenge to think about ministers rather than volunteers, don't be afraid to immerse yourself in the world of volunteer management. Just remember that everything you find there needs to be reworked into ministerial language. This means more than simply translating the vocabulary. It means always adding the faith development dimension to everything you do.

Begin with Robert Greenleaf's book *Servant Leadership* as a foundational document. If you are responsible for ministerial development, look also to Malcolm Knowles' book listed earlier. Make visits to your community's library and bookstores, both secular and religious. Do a Google search for "volunteer management" resources—you'll find more than you can ever use.

Develop Nurturing Structures for Ministers

The two primary implications of the faith development model proposed in this book are these.

- It is cyclical—constantly repeating itself on deeper and deeper levels—in a process that never ends.

- The first time around, each person walks the walk alongside another who acts as the guide. From then on, the person becomes the guide for others.

As a result, when planning support structures, the ministry director need look no further than the recognition that ministers are always on their own faith walks. The accumulation of successes and failures of life can bring even the most devout minister to great peaks and deep valleys, often at unlikely moments. As a result, always offer frequent opportunities for recharging, renewal, and refreshment to your ministers. (And, seek them for yourself as well.)

Later, in Chapter 14, the encounter on the road to Emmaus (Luke 24) is offered as the model for evangelization and catechesis. At the very heart of that encounter, Jesus listened to Cleopas and his friend. Later, after Jesus responded to them, they went off to spread the Good News they had received. In determining your approach to support for your ministers, look to that same model.

Look ahead also at Chapter 18 for thoughts on creating a work-pray-play balance in all that you do for ministers under your care. Let Jesus be your model. Strive for a whole-person balance for your ministers by offering them support structures that meet each of these three parts of life. And never forget to include spouses and families in the programs that you offer your ministers.

THE BIG QUESTIONS

While acknowledging that the Holy Spirit works in mysterious and surprising ways, try to lay out a systematic model of ministerial development for all those under your care. That is part of your responsibility as director or coordinator of pastoral ministers. Begin by thinking both in the short and long term. You might need to overload during the first year or two to cover the entire range of unmet needs among your ministers, but then look at events like annual or semi-annual retreats for ministers that might contain sequential themes so long-term ministers can stay constantly refreshed with new material. Remember always to balance between faith development and skill transmission. And always examine your plans with the work-pray-play balance in mind.

That having been said, what would your three- to five-year plan look like?

BIBLIOGRAPHY AND ASSOCIATED RESOURCES

Texas Instruments' commitment to volunteerism is legendary, going back nearly eighty years. It is a permanent part of their corporate culture. You can read more about it at their Web site: www.ti.com. I first discovered their work in this field in the mid-1960s, and it was already old news at that time.

Remembering that volunteer management concepts need to be translated into ministerial language, do a Google search for "volunteer management" or "volunteerism" resources—you'll find more than you can ever use.

Begin with the grandfather of andragogy. Amazon.com (www.amazon.com) has many titles by Malcolm Knowles, including the sixth edition of *The Adult Learner: A Neglected Species,* originally published in 1973.

A Google search on "andragogy" produced 107,000 references—enough to keep you busy for a while.

CHAPTER 8

Thank You, Thank You, Thank You

He sat down opposite the treasury, and watched the crowd putting money into the treasury. Many rich people put in large sums. A poor widow came and put in two small copper coins, which are worth a penny. Then he called his disciples and said to them, "Truly I tell you, this poor widow has put in more than all those who are contributing to the treasury. For all of them have contributed out of their abundance; but she out of her poverty has put in everything she had, all she had to live on."

Mark 12:41–44

We can never say "thank you" enough to parishioners. So often, we take lay ministers for granted. When you think you have said it enough, say it again. Say it from the pulpit. Say it at organization meetings. Say it in the bulletin. Say it in your annual report to parishioners. Say it at your "thank you" dinner for lay ministers that is put on by staff. Say it in personal messages. Say it in person. Say it in your one-on-ones. Never stop saying "thank you."

Remember always that parishioner gifts come in all forms—time, talent, and treasure. Especially in difficult economic times, many may have more time and talent than treasure to give. Ironically, those who find themselves giving of their time or talent may in fact be learning valuable lessons about the true nature of lay ministry in the church. Consequently, ministry leaders should always treat those gifts as having equal importance to that of treasure.

The first rule should be to offer genuine thanks to every donor, no matter the kind or size of gift. After all, the parish would fail if it were not for the generosity of **every** parishioner.

It may be obvious, but financial donors need to be thanked, person to person, however that can be done. The annual January tax letter is not enough—although it should be written in a way that says "thank you" first and then includes the specifics for tax deductibility. A one-to-one "thank you" on the church steps after Mass can do it. So can occasional telephone calls. One state park I go to has a commemoration plaque on every park bench and most trees. Another has similar bricks on a memorial walkway. Your parish has similar spots. It might be a special block of tiles in the gymnasium lobby, or chairs in the school library, or benches in the school yard. These can all be ways to thank donors. Don't wait for the annual donation letter to say "thank you" to all financial donors.

Every quarter, try sending more personalized versions of the annual income tax letter. Let donors know how their money is used by describing specific ministries of the parish in personal terms. Think about the advertisements on TV for child sponsorship agencies. They always send letters to donors with pictures of individual children and stories of their successes in different mission countries. Animal shelter organizations do the same things with pictures of dogs or cats that they have rescued. This approach is obviously successful, and we can learn from their experiences. If we appreciate pictures of dogs or cats, just imagine what a handwritten letter of thanks from the pastor might mean!

We must go further, however. Think outside the box and apply the same approaches to those who give of time and talent. Use your parish management software to track all contributions to ministries across the parish. Then, whenever letters are being sent to thank financial donors, do the same for the others.

Above all, these letters must be personalized. Even if the text of the letters is computer-generated, hand-written addenda at the bottom will go even further to let parishioners know that you are aware of their gifts and that you as the leader of the parish appreciate them.

Think about those who serve in key leadership positions—especially council and committee leaders. Purchase several copies of the best book you have read recently on an important ministerial issue. Use these moments of thanks to provide ministerial education as well by sending a copy to each member. Or, perhaps provide a one-year subscription to your favorite ministry magazine. Each issue will provide a tangible reminder of the appreciation you feel for them and will enhance their understanding of particular aspects of ministry. Isn't each member of your ministry team worth $19.95?

Make an annual Ministry Appreciation Dinner a major event. Invite by individual letters all those known to lead ministries, organizations, commissions, councils, and committees. Invite all liturgical ministers and all catechetical ministers. Invite coaches from the sports program. If your parish has a school, include their ministers as well. After all, it's one parish. Extend the invitation through the Sunday bulletin and pulpit announcements to all who have served the parish during the past year. Oh, yes, by the way: The staff should prepare and serve the food at this event.

One parish established an annual award for those whose ministry was *unique* (no one else was doing it), *ongoing* (each had been doing it for a long time), and *unnoticed* (each did it quietly in the background with no fanfare). Examples were the retired master cabinet maker, whose constructions for the parish, like the built-in trophy cases, were works of art, the retired man who opened the church each day at 4 AM and became an unpaid sacristan, and the woman who created a flower garden adjacent to the church building and tended it lovingly for years. When these individuals were honored at the annual "thank you" dinner, they received standing ovations from the parishioners. Perhaps they were not nearly as unnoticed as was thought.

Pick a "Ministry of the Month" for recognition on the home page of your Web site. Include lots of pictures. While the work of the ministry is important, the people doing it are more important. Recognize and say "thank you" to them. Be sure to keep doing this until you cover all parish ministries. Don't leave anyone out. Then do it again!

Use Sunday liturgies as prime opportunities for thanks—both through the pulpit and the bulletin. Regularly thank parishioners in the Sunday bulletin for extraordinary service. Particular ministry leaders can help the pastor identify these individuals. If this is done consistently, no one will be left out.

Ministry leaders can provide the pastor with three names each week of parishioners who ought to be thanked. Telephone calls or notes of thanks or just a brief encounter on the steps of the church following Sunday Mass will be noticed. Word will spread. Ministry leaders can themselves send personal "thank you" notes to key ministers. The parish staff and the pastoral council can easily play a major part in identifying such people and assisting with the task.

The Birthday Card Ministry described elsewhere can go a long way here. Put a hand-written note of thanks for the particular gifts that person has shared with the parish during the previous year.

Send occasional, spontaneous notes or e-mail messages.

"Last Thursday, I happened to notice you leading the choir rehearsal in the parish hall and was reminded of how effective you are in that ministry, and how devoted

you are to St. Brunhilde parish. I just wanted to take
a moment to thank you for your service. You help to
make this a great parish!"

The recipient is reminded that you know that person is there. In
a large parish, that is especially important.

THE BIG QUESTIONS

Do you express thanks for all gifts—those of time, of talent, and, or course,
of treasure?

How can we establish a broad, ongoing plan of thanks that can be built
into the work schedule so that it won't get lost in the shuffle of busy-ness
and always remain an "A" priority on the "To Do" list?

CHAPTER 9

Who Is the Most Important Person on the Staff?

> And everyone who has left houses or brothers or sisters or father or mother or children or fields, for my name's sake, will receive a hundredfold, and will inherit eternal life. But many who are first will be last, and the last will be first.
>
> Matthew 19:29–30

A Personal Story

My first professional job following college was in a large company in St. Louis. This was so long ago that the company still had elevator and switchboard operators. Within a few weeks of beginning there, I noticed the warm greeting that the old man at the front elevator gave to me and all employees each morning as we entered the building. He didn't always know our names, but he gave each of us a great "Hello" and a friendly smile. On the trip up the building, he would ask what department we were in, or what we did for the company. As he opened the elevator door and sent us off to our jobs, he always gave a cheery "Have a great day!" Each long distance call had to be placed through the telephone switchboard, and I soon learned that the operators were equally cordial. I didn't know their names, but they knew mine and greeted me personally each time I requested a call.

It occurred to me that these people were extremely important to the success of that company. Never mind that they were probably paid very little. They became the first contact with that company, whether by customer or employee, and the warmth of their greeting immediately set the tone for all additional dealings with others in the office. It is the reality of the importance of the first impression.

■ Who Is Important In Your Parish?

This is just as true for you today as it was for me forty-five years ago. Who are the most important members of your parish staff? They might just be the office receptionist, the parish janitor, the church sacristan, and the rectory housekeeper. Think about who sets the tone for that first encounter in your parish. Apply this checklist to your parish.

■ Who Greets Visitors?

In many city parishes, security concerns require that visitors be greeted through a window, perhaps one with iron bars on it, or through the use of a two-way intercom system. As necessary as these steps may be, they put up a wall of depersonalization between the visitor and the staff member that can only be overcome by the warmth that the receptionist uses in greetings. Are all reception staff trained in proper greeting procedures? Do they all understand the importance of this? Are they all on the same page?

If your parish is fortunate enough not to need such barriers, who opens the door when someone comes to the parish office? Must a visitor attempt to get the attention of the secretary? Is everyone greeted courteously, warmly, and with a smile? Do all reception staff members understand that each visitor is an occasion for ministry, and not an annoying interruption? What does the office look like? Is it well lit? Neat? Colorful? Friendly? Are there perhaps potted plants or seasonal decorations around the office? Will a visitor feel good about visiting the office? Is there a comfortable area for visitors with appointments in the office to sit?

Is frequently requested information—the weekly bulletin, applications to join the parish, informational flyers for religious education and other programs—available on a convenient rack?

If your parish plant is composed of several buildings, do you have a small, easy-to-understand map of the campus available for directing a first-time visitor?

Does your parish employ high school students as receptionists during evenings or weekends? If you do, for most, this will be their first job. They will be many guests' first encounter with the parish. Don't take for granted that they understand how to greet visitors, or the proper dress code for an office, or the proper type and volume of music that's OK in the office, or why it's not OK to use earphones in an office, or whether it is OK to do homework, or how to properly answer the telephone, or rules about Internet usage on office computers, or the inappropriateness of having buddies hanging around, or not throwing sharpened pencils at the ceiling so they stick in the acoustic tile. Help them learn these rules and skills with training, both before working and on the job.

Who gives out the key to meeting rooms in the evening? Is a proper balance struck between accountability for the key and a friendly greeting? Are evening receptionists provided with a list of all meetings scheduled for that night, including the name of the person delegated to receive the key? Are adequate and effective provisions made for conveniently returning the key later in the evening?

■ Who Answers the Telephone When Someone Calls?

Is the first contact when the telephone is answered *always* a real human being? (Save recorded messages, like the Sunday Mass schedule or directions to the church, as options to be requested, or for when someone calls in the middle of the night, when an emergency number can be given out.) How is the greeting? As with visitors, do all reception staff members understand that each telephone call is an occasion for ministry? Do they understand that some calls will be from people in distress? Is every call answered with a friendly tone of voice? Is there ever any impatience shown when trying to meeting the needs of the caller?

Here is a suggestion that you might never have thought of before. For several years, I recorded announcements called "continuity voice-overs" for the local cable channel. You hear these over the rolling screen credits at the end of a program. They are designed to keep you connected to the next program so you don't change channels. ("Be sure to stay tuned to discover the love life of the sea horse on the National Geographic special coming up next!") Even though these were audio announcements, and no one ever saw my face, I learned the importance of smiling while I read them! Believe it or not, it made a difference in how inviting and upbeat my message sounded. Encourage your telephone receptionists to do the same. It works!

Are telephone messages properly taken and accurately recorded? Try calling sometime. If your parish uses a computerized telephone answering system, remember what it feels like when you call your bank. Do not allow your parish telephone system to become a similar labyrinth of button options. *Never* request that callers "listen to the entire message because menu options have changed" or "your call is important to us." Everyone has become immune to those messages. They mean nothing to anyone. Don't use them.

■ Who Makes the Parish Look Good?

When a visitor or parishioner arrives, do the buildings and grounds look neat and well kept? Does the custodian look neat and well kept? Is sidewalk trash always picked up? Are garden spaces free of weeds? Is the grass regularly cut?

Are the office and other buildings well marked on the outside with clear signage? Is the office easy to find? If the office is in a different building from the rectory, is the distinction clear? Will an erroneous knock on the rectory door produce a friendly response with helpful directions to the office location?

Is the church sacristan dressed in a clean, appropriate manner and trained in proper greeting of visitors? After all, the sacristan may well be the first staff to meet visitors for weddings and funeral—visitors who may have no other contact with your parish. A moment of joy like a wedding can quickly turn sour if the visitor is poorly treated by the sacristan. Similar treatment can change a moment of sorrow at a funeral into one that convinces a visitor that churches are awful places. Their impressions of your parish are based in large part upon those encounters. A sacristan's curt treatment will completely negate the message of compassion or love in the homily.

■ Challenges for Others in Ministry Positions

As important as these first contacts are, all ministers in the parish share in the need to communicate the goals of the parish to everyone they meet. Everyone on the staff is a minister. The custodian might not see him/herself as a minister, but the ministry leader must help that person to share that responsibility. The frustration is that you will probably never know when opportunities for ministry occur. When the encounter is positive, it passes more or less as what is expected. When it is negative, the person may never return to the parish. In either case, it remains invisible to the ministry director.

Thus, if the custodian or sacristan or rectory housekeeper has been on the job for a very long time and has never been included in staff development activities, perhaps now is the time to do so. Include those staff in a day-long retreat to begin the new year. Include them in the staff "thank you" Christmas dinner. Ask the professional staff to affirm and encourage them for their work, especially the ministry of hospitality. It might be a new experience for them, but gradually it will occur to them that they are part of a team with a shared calling.

As was noted in another chapter, you never get a second chance to make a first impression.

First impressions mean everything!

THE BIG QUESTIONS

Identify those among the parish staff whom most people would consider least important. Often, they have worked for the parish for many years and are seen as fixtures there. Acknowledging that they often work alone and may be set in their ways, what can you do to include them in ministerial or staff gatherings? What can you do to help them see themselves as ministers and not merely employees?

CHAPTER 10

Help! We Need More Wall Space!
Celebrating Your Parish—Its Past, Present, and Future

So all the generations from Abraham to David are fourteen generations; and from David to the deportation to Babylon, fourteen generations; and from the deportation to Babylon to the Messiah, fourteen generations.

Now the birth of Jesus the Messiah took place in this way. When his mother Mary had been engaged to Joseph, but before they lived together, she was found to be with child from the Holy Spirit. Her husband Joseph, being a righteous man and unwilling to expose her to public disgrace, planned to dismiss her quietly. But just when he had resolved to do this, an angel of the Lord appeared to him in a dream and said, "Joseph, son of David, do not be afraid to take Mary as your wife, for the child conceived in her is from the Holy Spirit. She will bear a son, and you are to name him Jesus, for he will save his people from their sins." All this took place to fulfill what had been spoken by the Lord through the prophet: "Look, the virgin shall conceive and bear a son, and they shall name him Emmanuel," which means, "God is with us." When Joseph awoke from sleep, he did as the angel of the Lord commanded him; he took her as his wife, but had no marital relations with her until she had borne a son; and he named him Jesus.

Matthew 1:17–25

We live in a throwaway culture, in a world that values the new and innovative. We live at a time where change happens faster than we can process it. We are deluged by events, sometimes of staggering importance, but often we do not have time to process them before newer crises, equally overwhelming, overtake them and the earlier ones are buried in our memories. The past becomes relegated to very low importance. Yet, we stand on the shoulders of our past, of those who made the world what it is today—for better or for worse.

In our church, the past is our heritage and our tradition. Our stories are the basis of our faith. On the grand scale, those stories are commemorated in sacred books. We cherish and revere them. We have learned those stories since our earliest ages. At each eucharistic liturgy, we gather to celebrate our stories. Our church is built upon them.

On the local scale, we are not always so careful to commemorate our tradition. It is, however, equally important. What steps can we take as a local church to honor the gifts of our forebears?

Who were all the pastors of our church? Locate photographs of each one. (Your diocesan archivist can probably help.) Celebrate their contributions to your parish with a wall of photographs and biographies of each one, including the current one, perhaps in the vestibule of the church or in the parish office.

Develop the history of your parish. How did the parish begin? Was it originally a mission of an older parish? Who were the early parishioners, leaders, and donors? Whose names are commemorated on all the stained glass windows of the church? Who was the architect of the church building? What artists or artisans were instrumental in making your church a beautiful place? Was there an earlier church building, since demolished, where parishioners first gathered? Did the church move from an earlier location? Did the parish plant once look very different from the way it now looks? Ask some of the senior parishioners to bring in photos of parish life long ago and to write the history of your parish. Trying to put names on the faces on photos of Men's Club's Communion Sundays can stir many memories. Create a page on your Web site to tell the story. If it is a lengthy one, put one chapter at a time in the Sunday bulletin for the enrichment of parishioners. Help the newcomers and younger members share in the rich heritage of your parish. Help them share your pride. Help them remember your stories.

Find more wall space, or invest in stand-up easels. Develop walls of photos of past pastoral council leaders, current staff (with job titles), current pastoral council members (with titles), and current council and commissions.

Have a place for rotating photos of new parish families, this year's first communicants, confirmandi, and graduating classes. Have another for photos of recent major parish events.

If your parish has a building project underway or planned, a wall moving from the past through the present to the future could be very dramatic.

Flyers and posters for upcoming events should also have a prominent place.

(You might need to construct a new building for all the needed wall space!)

Obviously, not every parish has enough walls to do all these things. Perhaps your parish could rotate such displays. In any case, wall space is not the only way to honor your past. One parish created a memorial garden with commemorative bricks donated in the names of deceased parishioners. Another built a permanent book into the wall, a book made of metal pages commemorating important past contributors. Another created a very interactive history section of the parish Web site with lots of photos, audio interviews and video clips from parishioner home movies.

■ Saints and saints

Each day in the Roman Calendar, a saint is commemorated. Insert a weekly bulletin box with interesting information about one of the saints celebrated at a Mass this week. The lives of the saints can be very interesting, but most of us have probably not heard any of their stories since Sister read them to us in catechism class.

Saint Benedict should be remembered (July 11). As the father of monasticism, he placed supreme importance on the value of hospitality, a trait at the center of a great parish. Pope Paul VI made him the patron saint of Europe, since the monasteries he founded across the continent contributed to its early civilization after the fall of the Roman Empire.

Saints Peter and Paul ought to be celebrated, too (June 29), since they were the founders of the early church in Rome. It is on this day that each new archbishop receives his pallium (a special vestment representing the sign of his office) from the Holy Father.

Perhaps the others of the original eleven apostles ought also to be remembered in each parish, since they were the persons closest to Jesus.

Make All Saints Day a parish celebration. Who is the Patron Saint of the parish? Who are the Saints memorialized in the church stained glass? What do the parishioners know of these people? Celebrate each of these Saints on their feast days each year.

Ask parishioners to collectively identify the local saints of your parish. Celebrate the Saints and the saints. What does Sainthood mean? What does sainthood mean? One definition, remarkably similar to that of a hero, names a saint as one who does ordinary things in extraordinary ways. Perhaps the difference is that Saints do extraordinary things as well.

The Big Questions

Do you have enough wall space? If you don't, how can you properly honor your past and preserve its memory for all parishioners?

How can you clear some space in the vestibule to make room for such displays?

In your case, where is an equally appropriate place for these displays?

Does your parish office have, at the very least, wall photos of your pastor, your bishop and the pope?

CHAPTER 11

Readin', 'Ritin' and 'Rithmetic
Issues Unique to Parishes with Schools

The educational mission of the Church is an integrated ministry embracing three interlocking dimensions: the message revealed by God (*didache*) which the Church proclaims; fellowship in the life of the Holy Spirit (*koinonia*); service to the Christian community and the entire human community (*diakonia*). While these three essential elements can be separated for the sake of analysis, they are joined in the one educational ministry. Each educational program or institution under Church sponsorship is obliged to contribute in its own way to the realization of the threefold purpose within the total educational ministry....

To Teach as Jesus Did: A Pastoral Message on Christian Education,
Sec. 14, U.S. Conference of Catholic Bishops

Some pastors will thank God for the richness that a school brings to parish life. Others will thank God that they are not burdened with the obligation of maintaining a parish grade school.

Regardless of your position, if your parish has a school, there is no doubt that it brings with it an array of challenges not faced by parishes without them. What are some of those issues?

The elementary school is a major and vital ministry of the parish. It is arguably the largest, most organized ministry of the parish, perhaps even more so than Masses on Sunday.

The school is, in fact, a *ministry* of the parish. Unfortunately, many parishioners don't always see it that way.

The overriding issue is the pastor's attitude toward the school. While his attitude is the key factor in nearly every issue discussed in this book, there is no more important one than how he looks at the relationship between the parish and the school.

In busy churches, the parish and the school often have lives of their own. Each is a community with many members, and they share much in common, but if conscious effort is not exerted, they can drift apart—not unlike a married couple with two separate careers. "Conscious effort" seems to be the operative expression here. Structures and attitudes need to be present that value the larger community, especially for these reasons.

- The parish adult population is probably composed of a broader range of ages than that of the school. The parish includes many adults beyond child-rearing years, and the school does not.

- The major donors of the parish are probably its older members, since parents of school children are burdened with the expenses of their growing families and the not insignificant cost of tuition.

- The movers and shakers of the parish may be its older population as well, since they have the time to take on leadership roles.

■ The Big Picture

The Pastor and the Principal

Do the pastor and the principal share a common philosophy of Catholic education?

Do they share a common vision for the parish school?

Do the pastor and the principal meet regularly concerning parish issues affecting the school and school issues affecting the parish?

The Pastor and the Faculty

Does the pastor provide and personally direct a retreat for faculty members each year? Or does he participate with them in one led by a retreat director?

Does the pastor spend time with faculty members? Does he know each by name? Does he connect with each of them in any way beyond signing annual contracts?

The Pastor and the School

Does the pastor maintain a regular and frequent visible presence in the school, both with the students and with the faculty?

Does the pastor visit each classroom regularly?

Does the pastor teach any classes in the school, either ongoing or specially scheduled?

Does the pastor participate actively in meetings between the principal and parents concerning children with behavioral or serious academic problems?

The Parish and the School

How is school life incorporated into the broader life of the parish? Is the school an adjunct to or at the center of parish life?

Is there a place in the life of the parish for children and youth?

How relevant is the school to parishioners without children of school age?

Are schoolchildren visibly involved in parish liturgical activities?

How does the school's religion program interact with the parish's religious education program?

Are the sacraments of youth (First Communion, First Reconciliation, and confirmation) celebrated jointly or separately in the school and religious education programs? Acknowledging the differences between a 180-day-per-year school schedule and a once-a-week religious education schedule, what about the preparation programs?

Do parish high school students involve themselves in the life of the middle school so as to provide an easy transition when these children leave the school, such as serving as team members on middle school and confirmation retreats?

Does the school do any strategic or long-range planning? What are the population trends of the community? Is federal census data used to assist in this process? Can the leadership project with any level of certainty the short-, medium-, and long-term future of the school? Is this a shared process between the parish and the school?

Is the expectation that the parish will subsidize the financial operation of the school, or is the school self-supporting?

■ Some Specific Areas

What is the faculty years-of-service spread? Do the most senior teachers take advantage of opportunities to refresh and renew themselves, or are they stale or burnt out? Is there a balance of new, medium-duration, and long-term faculty? Does the faculty have a balanced male-female distribution?

What was the content of the last five in-service programs? Do all faculty members participate; or do senior teachers tend to excuse themselves from attending? Does any teacher never participate?

Are any teachers non-credentialed?

Does the school have a learning specialist on the faculty to work individually with children with special needs? After all, many children come to school with a great deal of "baggage" from home.

Are adjunct or support staff competent? Classroom aides? Specialty teachers? Extended care staff?

How is computer technology used in the school as a support to administration? Is there a school Web site? Can parents access homework assignments or grades on the Web site? Is the school schedule posted? Is the hot lunch menu posted? Do students have opportunities to contribute to the Web site?

How is technology taught? Does the school have a dedicated technology teacher? What grades are taught computer skills? How are computers used by teachers in classrooms? Does each teacher have a wireless laptop? How many computers does each classroom have? Does the school have a permanent computer lab room or does it have a rolling lab brought to each classroom with wireless laptops?

What are the enrollment trends? Are the upper grades full and the lower grades not so full, which is like a time bomb waiting to go off in a few years?

In how many of the last five years has the school operated with a balanced budget?

What are the school's non-tuition funding sources? Endowment income? Parent-Teacher Guild fund-raising? Benefactors? Foundations?

Is the Parent-Teacher Guild alive and well, offering support in non-financial ways?

THE BIG QUESTIONS

It might come as no surprise that these points were accumulated by asking several experienced principals what questions would be on the top of their lists if they were interviewing for new positions. It follows then that they ought also to be important to anyone seeking to improve the quality of school services. Apply them to your school. Be rigorous. If you don't know the answers, consult with the principal, the pastor, and any appropriate boards or commissions of the parish or school. Be sure to ask parents to answer those where they have some knowledge. What grade do you give yourself?

BIBLIOGRAPHY AND ASSOCIATED RESOURCES

To Teach As Jesus Did was a pastoral message issued by the U.S. bishops in 1972. A foundational and timeless document, it provided a framework for the themes of message, community, and service as integral elements of the educational ministry of the church. It encourages planning and collaboration in developing educational programs. It is available from the U.S. Bishops Conference Publishing Office (www.usccbpublishing. com). A Google search on the title produces over two million hits on related items, a testimony to this document's relevance and usefulness.

The Institute of School and Parish Development is a key source for free resources and valuable information. Go to its Web site (www.ispd.com) and check out the many papers in the Resource Center. Within that section, go to the Catholic School Enrollment Talks and download the August 2009 issue titled "Enrollment Questions You Should Ask as You Begin a New School Year" and the July 2007 issue titled "Helping School Secretaries Understand Their Role in Managing Enrollment" as excellent examples of their great work.

CHAPTER 12

Alumni Development
Another Issue Unique to Parishes with Schools

> The child grew and became strong, filled with wisdom;
> and the favor of God was upon him.
>
> Luke 2:40

The area of ministry most specifically related to schools is, of course, alumni development. Schools at every level, from elementary through post-graduate, possess a rich resource, which is only occasionally developed.

▨ A Personal Story

Several years ago, my mother responded to a bulletin article asking for the present addresses of grade school alumni. She completed the form on me and my three siblings and returned it to the school principal. Soon after that, I started to receive a great little newsletter from the old school. It always struck a balance between current news about the school, including lots of pictures and articles about events and student achievement, and news of alumni, where they were and what they were doing. Former students like me sent in old photos, and Sister published them all, with credit for the sources.

I faithfully read the entire newsletter, always searching for family names that I might remember. Periodically, I would be brought up to date on someone I hadn't seen in many decades. I loved it. In one issue, Dorothy, the school secretary, and her husband, Jerry, the basketball coach, were highlighted. I recalled a Dorothy and Jerry, members of my parish youth group many years before, who had dated. I immediately recognized their names—after all, there could only be one couple named Dorothy and Jerry, both Catholic, living in that small town—and telephoned the school. I had a wonderful reunion with two former kids whom I hadn't seen in many years. For several issues, the letter made no request for money, but always stapled to the center of the newsletter was a pull-out envelope, pre-addressed to the school, for the purpose of making a donation. As each issue arrived, I faithfully sent in a check, and I always received a gracious "thank you" letter in response.

After a while, Sister began to write about beginning an endowment fund. She told of the need for tuition assistance for families in that dying steel mill town, and I began to send in larger checks. So did many other alumni. Issue after issue, the fund grew. Once a year, Sister thanked all contributors by listing all their names.

After about seven years, the newsletters stopped. I never knew why. Perhaps Sister left that school. Who knows? All I knew was that when the newsletters stopped and the return envelopes stopped, I stopped giving. That was perhaps ten years ago, and I have never received another piece of mail from the old school.

There are lessons here.

- **When you ask, people will give.**
- **When you tell of specific needs, people will give more.**
- **When you stop asking, people will stop giving.**

When you work hard to develop good will and loyalty based upon a shared heritage, it will happen. What a tragedy for that school I mentioned earlier! For several years, they invested time, money and energy in developing a current alumni list. They worked hard to produce a quality informational piece. They faithfully held to a production schedule and sent newsletters out quarterly. (I eagerly awaited each one and was always delighted to receive it!) And their efforts seemed to be producing good results. But then they stopped. The huge investment they had made began immediately to lose value. As each month went by with no further mailings, two things happened. First, the accuracy of the mailing list quickly diminished for lack of follow-up. Second, the good will created with people like me began to evaporate. ("Out of sight, out of mind.") Over the years, I have often wondered why this happened.

Sister had reached out to me. I responded. Through the mailing piece, she offered a chance for me to reconnect with the school of my childhood. (After all, this was the place where in the fifth grade I had been a "Glory Be" in a Living Rosary! But that story will have to wait for another time.) Had I not lived two thousand miles away, I most certainly would have visited Sister and offered other services to the school. She had been effective in developing the alumni component around more than just giving. And then it vanished!

■ Be Faithful to Your School Graduates...

...and they will be faithful to you.

It is probably not necessary to lay out a rationale, but here are some important reasons for the importance of alumni development.

Many parishes pour major financial support into their schools. Beyond the money, schools significantly dominate parish life through the sheer numbers of people involved and the use of so many building resources during the school year. If you have any doubt, just recall the deafening silence that came over the plant the day after school closed for the summer!

As alumni mature into adults, most of them will look back fondly on their elementary school years. Alumni organizational contact motivates them to reconnect with this most important institution of their youth in many important ways.

- It invites them to share good memories with old friends and influential adults in their early lives.

- It provides a means for them to say "Thank you" to the people and place that helped make them the persons they have become. Many will express these thanks in both verbal and tangible ways.

- And, it serves as a moment of invitation towards evangelization and continuing faith development. Especially for the young adults only a few years removed from the grade school, it can work as a continuing connection to the faith that so many of them will step temporarily away from, returning perhaps only when they want to marry or baptize a first child.

- Older alumni are in a unique position springing from their loyalty to their alma mater to offer assistance through mentoring recent graduates and to encouraging younger alumni to stay connected and participate in reunions.

- Younger alumni can offer their services in after-school tutoring, help with extended care, and other adjunct programs.

Sister's work had not been haphazard. In retrospect, it is obvious that she had a plan, beginning with locating alumni.

Follow these steps for success in your school. Warning: it won't necessarily be easy, and it definitely won't be quick; and, to be successful, you will probably realize very quickly that you will need assistance, perhaps from one or more very dedicated graduates, to implement these steps. My personal story covered a period of seven years from the time my mother first gave Sister my name and address to the last newsletter I received.

■ Develop a Database of All Graduates

Start immediately. First, check the school's student management software to learn if it has an alumni module. You will save many hours of data entry if you utilize a program that already contains much of what you need and can exchange data between the main program and the alumni module. Since alumni development is based overwhelmingly on rekindling the relationship with former students, select a database program that offers field creation that meets your present and future needs. Name, address, telephone, e-mail, occupation, graduation year, parents, gifts and talents, links to siblings, event participation history, donation history, e-commerce, salutation options, and easy mail merge capability—these are all essential features. Do a Google search on "alumni management software," and a review of available products will give ideas about what the potential is. Realize at the outset that the field is dominated by products aimed at college and university alumni. You will need to sort through the data to find those that aim at elementary schools.

Alumni management is a lucrative computer software field. It is a very desirable product because school development offices realize that alumni can become a source of significant contributions to a school and are willing to pay for products that will enhance that effort. These packages fall into two categories.

- Stand-alone software applications are more economical. You purchase the package, install it on your own computer or network, and start using it.

- Web-based applications are more like subscriptions to an ongoing service. Your school enters into an agreement with a company, enters all data into their computer system (via the Internet), and uses their services. This method can be much more expensive, potentially involving both a start-up cost and a monthly or annual cost per student, but their services frequently go far beyond what a stand-alone package can do. You may find that this approach is more appropriate for colleges and universities and exceeds the scope of your elementary school's alumni work.

You will need to go further than a simple Excel file database that contains names, addresses, and year of graduation. Other features you will find useful might include ability to import Excel data, e-mail addresses, multiple address per student (home, college, work), links to siblings who share the same parent, user-defined salutations for merge letters, tracking of degree and accomplishment history, tracking of student clubs, activities and awards, alumni event participation history, donation history, easy ability to set up an "Endowment Fund" pledge system (if you were to reach that point), marital status, spouse information, ability to attach any type of document scan to an individual's record (newspaper article, image, etc.), free-form comments field, ability to reach an individual's parents, areas for "Friends of Your School" and present and former faculty.

Once you have selected the appropriate software package, begin the process of entering every name of every graduate—living and dead, from this year all the way back to the first graduating class of the school. Why deceased graduates? Because later, when you are assembling class lists, graduates will still want to remember those who have died. You will be able to extract data from the school's student management software for recent graduates, but you will probably need to look at paper records for earlier classes. If individual student records can't be used, look at the class photos that probably hang on the walls of your school. Then the task will be to find addresses. Beyond those available from the school computer, look to parish records, since most students were children of parish families. Involve veteran parishioners and faculty members as your "historical consultants." (Everyone loves a title!) Every parish and school has those people who have been around for a long time and knew everyone. Use the parish bulletin as a vehicle to get location information. It's a great way to reach many parishioners.

By the way, get e-mail addresses on everyone in every request for information you make. Incorporate e-mail address requests into *all* regular school mailings as well. Yes, e-mail addresses change frequently. Yes, maintenance of your list is a nuisance task. But, e-mails are *free* to send, unlike a mailed letter, which now approaches fifty cents for postage alone. And younger people are completely immersed in e-mail over snail mail.

■ Involve the Parish from the Beginning

Successful alumni development is built upon a positive pastoral relationship between the parish and the school. Make certain that the pastor and the principal share similar answers to these questions.

- What can we do so that the school is seen as a major, vital ministry of the parish?

- How can we create better links between parish life and school life?

- What can we do to better connect school families with parish life?

- What can we do to eliminate any apparent gaps between the church and the school?

Meet with the parish and school staffs to cover the same questions. Meet with the pastoral council to bring its members up to date on alumni development plans. Always look for opportunities for better church-school cooperation.

Begin a long-term campaign to invite and involve the priests, staff, and pastoral council members into school life—in any way you can think of. To paraphrase the words of one pastor, "Love them into embracing the school!"

Look to current and past parish leaders who are school graduates.

Look to the high school youth ministry program in the parish, since many members will be graduates of the school.

The ability to reach the larger parish community easily, especially at weekend Masses, is critical. Make certain that you have good communications with parish staff regarding bulletin articles, inserts, and pulpit announcements. Produce a weekly "School News" bulletin insert. Prepare other bulletin announcements requesting alumni current addresses and e-mail addresses. Create Class-by-Class bulletin inserts that focuses on "Where have all our classmates gone?"

Meet with all parish organizations to locate alumni and invite involvement.

■ Involve Your Eighth-Graders before They Graduate

The best time to encourage lifelong alumni connections is when they are still students in the school. Throughout the year, regularly involve eighth-graders in hosting responsibilities for any alumni meeting or event held in the school. Use them, for instance, as hosts for an alumni tour of the school.

In the days just before graduation, and during graduation activities, take the following steps.

- Meet with present eighth-graders. Get e-mail addresses and high school information from each one. Share information about the alumni association with them.

- Ask class members to elect alumni officers who can head up work on their first-year reunion to be held the next year.

• As part of graduation activities, include a formal induction into the Alumni Association and present each graduate with a class name-and-address directory as a memento. Present each with an Alumni Association card with free membership during their high school and college years.

■ Enlist the Support of Neighboring Parishes

Enlist the support of neighboring parishes that feed your school and Catholic high schools that accept many of your graduates.

While cooperation with other parishes for bulletin articles can sometimes be spotty, try to get names and e-mail addresses of all bulletin editors. Ask other parishes to announce your plans for alumni and request names and addresses of any graduates of your school. Send bulletin article requests by e-mail, with a suggestion to "cut and paste," thus eliminating the need to retype an item. You might get better results.

Look to all the Catholic high schools with your graduates for help, both to identify potential alumni members through the meetings described below, and for regular announcements about alumni events and activities. Seek assistance from campus ministers or religion teachers to identify your graduates and update addresses. Ask to meet with your grads to invite their involvement. Identify a key student at each high school who can be your connection. Send occasional requests for announcements about alumni events, or articles for school newspapers about alumni activity by their students.

■ Form an Alumni Planning Committee, Leading to an Alumni Association

Form a group of key alumni to take ownership of this process and assist with advice and help in the development of all that you do. Alumni activity needs to be as much their work as yours. Recruit chairpersons for each class or, in the case of older classes, clusters of classes, who can continue to take the lead in locating graduates and can help promote reunion events. Decide whether there would be value in a connection between an alumni association and the parent-teacher organization. Ask them to decide on questions like association membership and whether or not to charge dues, an association title, logo, frequency of social activities, and the like.

◼ Add an Alumni Page to the School Web site

Initially, just a single page will probably be enough, announcing formation of the alumni development effort, a link button to send in e-mail addresses, and an early invitation to any all-alumni events.

As alumni efforts begin to happen, a separate alumni Web site can be offered, with a separate page for each class. Scan and include class photos. Always ask the question "Where have all our classmates gone?" Request updates on present location and e-mail addresses. Strive for interactivity, lots of stories and photos from alumni, and the ability to make donations with credit cards.

Make video recordings of graduations and major school events. Produce tightly edited shows that can be seen on the Web site.

Record interviews with all living past principals and veteran teachers. Offer as podcasts on the Web site.

Think about using social networking Internet communities, like Facebook, YouTube, and Twitter. Many alumni are very computer-literate. Provide blogging opportunities for storytelling, where one person can build on the story begun by another. This author has found Facebook indispensable in locating alumni of the parish school, as literally hundreds of graduates are connected to Epiphany-related sections of that network.

Ask the parish Web site to include a link button to an alumni page. Offer to do the same for the parish Web site on the alumni site.

■ Send an Alumni Newsletter

First, cultivate relationships. Later, ask for money. Make that the mantra of all your alumni development efforts, but particularly your alumni newsletter.

Some hallmarks of alumni newsletters.

- Ask a graphic artist to design an eye-catching layout for you right at the beginning. You can then use it as a template for each issue. Always make certain that your computer spell-checker is on. Make certain that each issue is reviewed by another person, checking both for the quality and clarity of the written word and for errors in grammar or spelling. Spell-checkers won't find every error, especially when the misspelled word is actually another correctly spelled word (like "Patent-Teacher Guild")! And, no matter how thorough you are, you can't proofread your own work! Use photos that are crisp, clear, and show faces. Let your alumni be proud of the quality work you are doing, just for them!

- Strike a balance between current school news and updates about former students. Alumni love to read about how their old school has grown and matured! And they love to spot names and faces of former classmates from their own eras.

- Honor an "Alumnus of the Month." Pick someone whose success includes ongoing parish or school involvement.

- Use lots of pictures—pictures of smiling students and smiling alumni.

- Give lots of information about upcoming reunions and other alumni events.

- Always include a section on identifying alumni who are "missing in action." Many times, former students will know where classmates have moved. Even with only a city known, online white pages can help you find them.

- Highlight your class chairpersons. Give them opportunities to write short pieces about development with their classes.

- Give thought to how you make requests for donations.

- Invite recipients to choose to receive the newsletter as a PDF file e-mail attachment, thus saving postage costs.

- Always use "ADDRESS SERVICE REQUESTED" on the outside of each mailing. (Check with your local post office to get instructions on the proper way to do this.) That way, when a recipient's address has changed, the U.S.P.S. will notify you of the correction—for a small fee. It's worth the cost to help keep your mailing list accurate. Address changes recorded with the postal service have an expiration period, usually six months. If you send mailings more frequently than that with this notation on the envelope, you are assured of getting information about every move.

■ Have a High-Visibility Kickoff Event, Like a Homecoming

Strategically, this should be a very important, high-visibility event. In the invitation, ask if child care services would be needed. One parish chose to have an all-class reunion during the Christmas break so they could reach college students home for the holidays. The event you choose could be anything from an informal social gathering to a sit-down dinner. Either way, offer lots of ways for participants from individual classes to reconnect. Invite former faculty members, principals, and parish priests with school connections. Keep the speeches brief, but introduce the Alumni Association leadership and let everyone know about future events. Invite volunteers for individual class chairpersons. Consider offering a tour of the school.

For this first event, most attendees will probably be graduates from recent years, since you are more likely to know their addresses. Invitations to older alumni will have been mailed to parents, and you should encourage them to share the invitation with their alumni.

Ongoing Alumni Contact

The first goals of alumni development will be to re-establish contact with former students and to cultivate relationships with them. Requests for donations will happen in due time.

Use all contacts to invite alumni to serve as class (or class clusters) chairpersons. Always get all information on alumni location and status.

Work to get alumni back on campus. Always invite connections. Occasionally, incorporate tours of the school into on-campus events. Regularly invite alums to school events, like First Communions, confirmations, and graduations (both eighth-grade and kindergarten). Invite a successful alumnus to speak at the graduation ceremony. Ask alumni to assist with open houses for prospective new school families.

Continue to Host One Annual All-Class Homecoming Event

At one school, the kickoff event, an all-class reunion held during the Christmas break, was so well received that many alumni asked for it to be continued as an annual event. Overall, ongoing development work had resulted in many classes holding their reunions and rediscovering their own class spirit, but the homecoming event became the premier fundraiser for the school. Each year the school presented the "Alumnus/Alumna of Distinction" award to an outstanding former student.

Assist Classes with Reunions

First, the School Alumni Development Office should offer major organizational support for reunion planning. While the event belongs to the class, the school administrative resources can offer the support that class leaders will need to help make the event a success. One school offers a helpful "How to Plan a Reunion" brochure.

Second, the school should encourage and plan *annual* reunions in the four years following graduation for these reasons.

- Graduates still have a great deal in common from their recent years together at your school.

- They are continuing to have similar experiences as high school students, and will have a lot to share with one another.

- Annual reunions will keep their connections to your parish and school strong from the very beginning, thus encouraging more faithful alumni involvement in future years.

Beyond the first four years out, reunions are more likely to occur at five- or ten-year intervals. As graduates mature into adulthood, decisions about frequency of reunions and who will run them belong more and more to each class leadership. As classes reach twenty or more years since graduation, reunions can become weekend festivals, including perhaps an informal hotdog barbecue on Friday evening or Saturday afternoon, a tour of the school hosted by eighth-graders, a formal dinner on Saturday evening, and a parish Mass either on Saturday before the dinner or on Sunday morning where alumni can be recognized and honored.

One school holds special reunions for graduates of fifty years ago, where "Golden Diploma" memberships are awarded.

■ Continue to Research the History of the School

The goal here is to humanize the school's history with many names and faces, which will bring it home to the reader. In many parishes, the history has already been written for earlier commemorations, which can be used as starting points needing updating. Try to identify all past principals (with their years of service), parish priests who had school involvement, and, if possible, a listing of all past faculty members. Humanize the history by inviting stories from alumni. Ultimately, place the school's history on the school, alumni, and parish Web sites.

THE BIG QUESTIONS

The importance of a major commitment from those in development leadership cannot be overstated. Who are the key people in your school's history to serve in such roles? Look especially for those who have had continuing involvement in both parish and school life.

What kind of administrative support from school staff can be offered?

BIBLIOGRAPHY AND ASSOCIATED RESOURCES

The Institute of School and Parish Development (www.ispd.com) offers great resources for alumni development. Again, check out the Resource Center of their Web site and look at the resource paper titles. Frank Donaldson, the president of this company and its chief visionary, knows what he is talking about. His papers offer solid information and challenging questions for reflection.

These social networking Web sites have found their way into nearly every aspect of today's world. Become familiar with them and learn to use them. Understand both the downsides and upsides of these phenomena.
www.facebook.com
www.myspace.com
www.youtube.com
www.twitter.com

CHAPTER 13

Green: An Extraordinary Color

Grateful for the gift of creation...we invite Catholics and men and women of good will in every walk of life to consider with us the moral issues raised by the environmental crisis....These are matters of powerful urgency and major consequence. They constitute an exceptional call to conversion. As individuals, as institutions, as a people, we need a change of heart to preserve and protect the planet for our children and for generations yet unborn.

Renewing the Earth, United States Catholic Conference

Green is more than the liturgical color of Ordinary Time. "Going Green" has developed into the catchphrase for the environmental movement today. Almost everyone has become more sensitized to the effects of global warming and the trashing of the earth. This is increasingly true for both individuals and institutions.

Can there be anything more appropriate for parish involvement than fostering stewardship for the earth? Why has it taken so long for churches to acknowledge this issue? Long before churches were speaking of stewardship, environmentalists advocated it. Thankfully, many Christian churches, especially evangelical ones, have finally recognized it as an appropriate moral issue demanding a response. We have only one earth. God gave it to us. We must cherish it and leave it better than we found it.

The parish is in a unique position to respond to environmental concerns. First, the parish as a large physical entity can implement steps within its own plant and in its own operations. By doing so, it not only reduces its own environmental impact but it also models new behavior that parishioners can learn. Second, the parish has the ability to reach, sensitize, and mobilize its many families into responsive action. Each of these points is considered separately below.

■ Environmental Changes in the Parish

Buildings and Grounds

First, before anything else, enlist the support of the custodians and sacristans of the parish and school. Their involvement in all aspects of both recycling and energy conservation will be critical to your success.

Check with your trash removal service to see if recycling is possible. In many cities, they provide separate containers for trash and for recycling. (Some even add a third for composting.) Some also give discounts for recycling because the amount of landfill-directed trash is reduced. Recycle paper, cans, glass, plastic, and whatever else your scavenger service will permit. Remember to recycle out-of-date missalettes and songbooks. They may constitute the single largest amount of paper you discard at any one time, If it is possible in your church building, consider projecting music on screens during liturgies and eliminating printed song sheets.

Conduct a survey across the entire parish plant for lead paint, treated lumber, and other hazardous substances, especially around play structures, and then develop a systematic plan to remove them.

Ask your power utilities to conduct energy audits of all your buildings. Using their advice, set an energy reduction goal and ask everyone using parish facilities to help meet it. Ask them also about lighting retrofits.

Check your buildings for adequate insulation so that expensive heat or cooling is not leaking from them. Insulation improvement can be a cost-effective way to save on heating and cooling costs.

Install weatherstripping and caulking on openings with drafts.

Parishes can purchase and use non-toxic cleaning products.

Use unbleached, environmentally friendly paper towels and tissue in bathrooms.

Does everyone understand the essential relationship between animals and plants? Animals (including human beings, of course) require oxygen and produce carbon dioxide. Plants require carbon dioxide and produce oxygen. You can't have one without the other. Each produces what the other consumes. Trees are the best oxygen producers because they are big. Look around your parish property. Where can you plant more trees or shrubs? Where can you install a garden?

Consider having solar panels (either photo-voltaic to produce electricity or solar hot water) installed on building roofs. These can produce dramatic reductions in electric and heating bills.

Consider green roofs on flat surfaces. This will help reduce toxic runoff into storm drains and reduce heating costs in warmer climates.

Office and Kitchens

Use e-mail to communicate wherever possible and avoid using paper.

Include a second wastebasket for paper to be recycled by each desk in the parish office.

Buy and use recycled paper. Then recycle it again when you dispose of it.

Rectories can begin to compost kitchen waste.

Rectories can start vegetable gardens in their back yards.

"Energy Star" is a title given by the Environmental Protection Agency to appliances that meet its energy-saving standards. Most consumers have heard it mentioned in commercials, as manufacturers boast when their models receive the designation. The EPA maintains a Web site called Energy Star for Congregations that gives much more information, claiming that churches can save as much as thirty percent by investing strategically in efficient equipment, facility upgrades, and maintenance.

The Energy Star program also gives recognition for congregational energy efficiency upgrades. They provide a Portfolio Manager tool to record "before and after" energy amounts. This document will be helpful in learning the amount of your church's energy savings whether you enter the EPA's award program or not.

Learn about "Energy Star" appliances when it is time to purchase new ones. Ask about available rebates.

Clean refrigerator coils twice a year and check that refrigerator door seals are intact so the doors close tightly. Use the dollar bill test. Slip a dollar bill between the door frame and the seal. If it easily pulls out, the seal may need to be replaced.

Make sure that all air conditioning units are free of any obstruction so they work efficiently.

Parishes with kitchen facilities can incorporate composting into their recycling plans. Organic waste, such as clippings and leaves, can also be composted.

Reduce landfill trash by using compostable paper plates and not plastic for picnics, parties, and social events.

Churches can buy and use organic produce at parish events, including fair trade coffee. Posters or signs near food service lines announcing this policy can help educate church members.

HVAC

Invest in annual check-ups of your heating, ventilating, and air conditioning (HVAC) equipment. Consider annual maintenance contracts.

Purchase and use newer thermostats that allow you to set times for different days of the week when heating is used.

Consider locking covers for thermostats in public spaces so changes can be made only by authorized persons.

Keep furnace filters clean, which will result in cleaner air and lower heating costs.

Lighting

Parishes can install timers and motion detectors for lighting across the plant.

Replace all incandescent light bulbs with compact fluorescent lights (CFLs). Popular demand has brought prices down significantly. New technology in their production provides different bulbs with different light tones that eliminate the former complaint that they make everything look greenish. It is claimed that replacing just one sixty-watt incandescent light bulb with a CFL will save thirty dollars over the life of the bulb. CFLs also last ten times longer than incandescent bulbs, use two-thirds less energy, and give off seventy percent less heat. If every U.S. family replaced one regular light bulb with a CFL, ninety billion pounds of greenhouse gases would be eliminated, the same as taking 7.5 million cars off the road.

Ask your electrical supplier to provide information about newer four-foot and eight-foot tubular fluorescent bulbs and ballast improvements as well.

Change exterior lighting used for parking lots and other security to more efficient metal halide or high-pressure sodium fixtures. These new technology light sources are compact, powerful, and efficient. Use timers and photocells for outdoor lighting as well.

Use newer LED exit signs that consume only tiny amounts of electricity.

Water

Use insulated blankets on all water heaters to help reduce heat loss. Special insulated wrap should also be used on the first six feet of hot water supply pipe coming from the heater. In fact, many municipalities require this by code on new installations.

Review all water usage. Many water companies or districts will tell you what your usage is in one year compared to the last.

Locate and fix leaky faucets and pipe fittings.

Install faucet aerators and low-flow showerheads.

Put timers on sprinklers so they work at night and reduce evaporation from sunlight.

Eliminate the use of plastic bottled water at parish meetings, in the parish office and in the rectory. Use water pitchers instead.

Use native plants in parish gardens or other landscaped areas. They almost always use less water than more exotic plants.

Vehicles

Make mass transit information available to parishioners to reduce automobile use getting to Sunday Masses.

Determine if there is interest in providing carpool matching service for parishioners for Sunday Mass.

If the parish or school owns any automobiles, consider hybrids and other low-emission/high-mileage vehicles.

■ Bringing Parishioners to an Environmental Sensitivity through Education and Advocacy

Use each step described above as a "teachable moment," always sharing with parishioners the steps being taken to help the parish become better stewards of the earth. Remind them, too, that these steps save parish money, which, after all, is their money!

Some states, like California, have organizations directed toward churches and other non-profits for the purpose of making public declarations or covenants of policy to support environmental stewardship and sustainability. Check out www.interfaithpower.org. They can be helpful when your church wants to announce publicly its position on this issue of worldwide importance. Check the Internet to see if your state or city has such a group. Google for "environmental covenant." Even if no such organization exists for your area, your church can still make such a statement on your own. The covenant found on the Web site shown above is a great starting point. You don't really need to send it anywhere. Start by asking your pastoral council to approve it as parish policy. That action can be publicly endorsed by the pastor at all Sunday Masses, perhaps just before Earth Day. Then, appoint a council committee to become lead agents in implementing it. All these steps should be done before the assembly so your church members know about it and can do the same in their own homes.

On Earth Day 2009, many Catholics participated in the "Take the St. Francis Pledge" movement, a program created by the Catholic Climate Covenant and supported by many bishops and the U.S. Conference of Catholic Bishops. Families signing the pledge agreed to:

- PRAY and reflect on the duty to care for God's Creation and protect the poor and vulnerable.

- LEARN about and educate others on the causes and moral dimensions of climate change.

- ASSESS how we—as individuals and in our families, parishes and other affiliations—contribute to climate change by our own energy use, consumption, waste, etc.

- ACT to change our choices and behaviors to reduce the ways we contribute to climate change.

- ADVOCATE for Catholic principles and priorities in climate change discussions and decisions, especially as they impact those who are poor and vulnerable.

It is unknown at the time of this writing whether or not this will become an annual event. The concept remains valuable for parishioner education and personal action and could be used even without institutional support.

Parishes can join in community-wide celebration of Earth Day held around the world each year on April 22. Hold an environmental fair on the Sunday before with resources available for parishioner action.

Parish groups can host environmental stewardship presentations at meetings.

Priests and deacons can begin to include environmental stewardship issues within homilies, helping to bring more and more parishioners to understand the moral imperative of this issue.

Sponsor a composting workshop for interested families. Some cities offer discounted compost bins. Parishes could host such a service, thus helping their cities to reduce the amount of refuse in the waste stream. Families will be amazed to see how much organic waste goes into a compost bin and not into the garbage can.

Provide brochures about energy audits and environmental resources for parishioners on information racks, at group meetings, or at annual environmental events.

Consider allowing community vegetable gardening on unused portions of parish land. Encourage parishioners to plant vegetables there and share in the bounty of the earth.

Parish grade schools have an incredible opportunity to reach children and their families. Children are particularly open to learning how to save the earth. Make sure that the religious education program does the same thing for public school children.

THE BIG QUESTIONS

A parish is in a unique position to become an agent of change for concern for the earth. Is your parish ready to make stewardship for the earth part of your "way of doing business?"

How will your parish create an environmental covenant? What will it promise? What kind of leadership structure will you add to see that it remains an important goal for your parish?

Consider each of the two purposes of this chapter separately.

- To reduce your parish's own environmental impact and, by doing so, to model new behavior that parishioners can learn, and
- To reach, sensitize, and mobilize your many families into their own responsive action.

How can you project a program for change in both these areas, understanding that they require a change in thinking and will probably take some time?

How will you be able to measure success in these many areas?

BIBLIOGRAPHY AND ASSOCIATED RESOURCES

Go to www.energystar.gov/congregations. You will find lots of unbiased information and access to other Web sites to carry your interest in energy reduction and related issues even further. Go to www.energystar.gov/benchmark to download the Portfolio Manager Tool.

Go to www.interfaithpower.org to download the Congregational Covenant (in English or Spanish) if your parish wants to make a public declaration of your intentions in environmental reform. Nothing there is etched in stone. Use their covenant as is, or as a starting point for your own parish version. The important thing is to take a stand.

Also, go to www.catholicclimatecovenant.org for another view developed in part by the U.S. Catholic Bishops Conference on this same movement.

CHAPTER 14

Do You Know the People in Your Pew?
In-Reach

But wanting to justify himself, he asked Jesus, "And who is my neighbor?" Jesus replied, "A man was going down from Jerusalem to Jericho, and fell into the hands of robbers, who stripped him, beat him, and went away, leaving him half dead. Now by chance a priest was going down that road; and when he saw him, he passed by on the other side. So likewise a Levite, when he came to the place and saw him, passed by on the other side. But a Samaritan while traveling came near him; and when he saw him, he was moved with pity. He went to him and bandaged his wounds, having poured oil and wine on them. Then he put him on his own animal, brought him to an inn, and took care of him. The next day he took out two denarii, gave them to the innkeeper, and said, 'Take care of him; and when I come back, I will repay you whatever more you spend.' Which of these three, do you think, was a neighbor to the man who fell into the hands of the robbers?" He said, "The one who showed him mercy." Jesus said to him, "Go and do likewise."

Luke 10:29–37

◼ A Personal Story

Many years ago, while still in diocesan work, I was asked to attend a youth ministry planning meeting at a parish in Schenectady, New York. It was a Sunday morning—this happened to be that Sunday in January when we used to celebrate ecumenism. I had forgone Sunday Mass at my own parish in favor of attending there, so as to get a flavor of parish life. A neighboring Protestant minister was there to share a message with the parishioners. At the end of Mass, a couple in my pew approached me. We had just a few minutes before exchanged the Sign of Peace. "Who are you?" the husband asked. "We knew you weren't a parishioner because we hadn't seen you here before. But you didn't come with the visiting minister because you knew all the responses." His wife obviously shared this moment of curiosity. I was amazed! After recovering from my shock, I explained to them why I was there that morning. We shared names and coffee with one another before I excused myself to get to the intended meeting.

I have never forgotten than moment. Wouldn't it be wonderful (and extraordinary) if we knew the others in our own pew (or even a few pews around us!) so well that we would notice a stranger in our midst! Are our parishes so big that such a dream seems unreachable? A "Yes" to that question might give the first clue about change needed in our parishes: change in the direction of Small Christian Communities. I suspect, however, that such depersonalization exists even in small parishes.

◼ Talking and Listening

While Chapter 15 covers communication of important information to parishioners and Chapter 16 deals with outreach to the unchurched, this one has to do with reaching those who are already in the parish, the active, the inactive, the nominal, and the invisible—and doing most of it *in person*! Call it in-reach. The difference between this chapter and the next is simple. Here, we are talking about listening to the parishioners. In the next chapter, it's about talking to them. How do parish ministers reach out to or respond to both the visible and invisible members of the parish?

No single story from the New Testament illustrates the way Jesus responded to people more than the encounter on Easter Sunday afternoon on the road to Emmaus.

> Now on that same day two of them were going to a village called Emmaus, about seven miles from Jerusalem, and talking with each other about all these things that had happened. While they were talking and discussing, Jesus himself came near and went with them, but their eyes were kept from recognizing him. And he said to them, "What are you discussing with each other while you walk along?" They stood still, looking sad. Then one of them, whose name was Cleopas, answered him, "Are you the only stranger in Jerusalem who does not know the things that have taken place there in these days?" He asked them, "What things?" They replied, "The things about Jesus of Nazareth, who was a prophet mighty in deed and word before God and all the people, and how our chief priests and leaders handed him over to be condemned to death and crucified him. But we had hoped that he was the one to redeem Israel. Yes, and besides all this, it is now the third day since these things took place. Moreover, some women of our group astounded us. They were at the tomb early this morning, and when they did not find his body there, they came back and told us that they had indeed seen a vision of angels who said that he was alive. Some of those who were with us went to the tomb and found it just as the women had said; but they did not see him." Then he said to them, "Oh, how foolish you are, and how slow of heart to believe all that the prophets have declared! Was it not necessary that the Messiah should suffer these things and

then enter into his glory?" Then beginning with Moses and all the prophets, he interpreted to them the things about himself in all the scriptures. As they came near the village to which they were going, he walked ahead as if he were going on. But they urged him strongly, saying, "Stay with us, because it is almost evening and the day is now nearly over." So he went in to stay with them. When he was at the table with them, he took bread, blessed and broke it, and gave it to them. Then their eyes were opened, and they recognized him; and he vanished from their sight. They said to each other, "Were not our hearts burning within us while he was talking to us on the road, while he was opening the scriptures to us?" That same hour they got up and returned to Jerusalem; and they found the eleven and their companions gathered together. They were saying, "The Lord has risen indeed, and he has appeared to Simon!" Then they told what had happened on the road, and how he had been made known to them in the breaking of the bread. (LUKE 24:13–35)

In this encounter, Jesus *asked* what they were discussing. He *listened* carefully to their reply. He *responded by interpreting* through Scripture the meaning of the events. *Mutual sharing* continued. They recognized him in the *breaking of the bread*. They in turn went off the *spread the Good News* they had received.

At the heart of the story is *listening*. These two, Cleopas and his friend, had been followers of Jesus. They were open to him and his message. They believed him to be the Messiah, but the events on Friday had dealt a crushing blow to their hopes and aspirations. They had not yet, after all, come to understand what had happened on Easter morning. After meeting them on the road, Jesus had nothing to say until he had listened to them. Only after he understood the turmoil, the confusion, the disappointment they felt, did he utter a word. Even after everything, they were open to and listened to him, this stranger who had appeared in their midst. His interpretation of the words of Scripture apparently made sense to them, because they invited him to come in. They obviously wanted more. They invited Jesus in, Jesus didn't force his way. Then, they allowed him to become the host. He, this stranger in their midst, offered the blessing and broke the bread—a most extraordinary reversal of traditional roles. Only then, by permitting the tables to be turned, did they recognize him. They were so excited that they had to run and tell others of what had just happened to them! Jesus' resurrection had immediately become the central element of Christian belief. It was not a peripheral issue. From that moment forward, it was the central driving force. It animated the believers instantly.

The Emmaus encounter has become the model for evangelization and catechesis because more today than ever before it calls upon us to first listen and only then respond. The dialogue springs from the **needs of the learner** and not the **agenda of the teacher**.

Most parishes are successful to varying degrees in maintaining a mailing list, in producing a readable Sunday bulletin, and, most important, in getting offertory envelopes into the hands of parishioners. Many have a Web site and are good at answering e-mails.

The place where most parishes fail, however, is in genuine, sustained human-to-human contact. It is just *so* time-consuming. Of course, the irony of the modern age is that most people are starving for such contact. How much junk mail hits our mailbox? How many e-mail messages do we receive each day? Even with good spam filtering, we drown in the sea of print communication. We don't need any more.

What each of us appreciates is an authentic personal connection—one where I am the center of another's attention, without interruption by cell phone or another person. What if we found that within our parish? What a rare moment that would be. Several ideas for in person people-to-people contact are described below.

■ What the Parish Can Do

Name Tags, Coffee, and Doughnuts after Sunday Mass
Coffee with absolutely no agenda other than to meet and listen to parishioners. No selling of anything. No appeal for larger donations. Just: "Thank you for belonging to this parish. Thank you for coming this morning." Do this once a month after the Sunday Mass with enough time before the next one so that the parking lot doesn't get overloaded. Have name tags and introduce new families to everyone. Perhaps once every three months, invite brief sharing, like "What do you wish the parish would be? What do you wish the parish would do more or less of?" Why not use that Sunday as a monthly opportunity for everyone to wear name tags at Mass? Before Mass begins, invite everyone to introduce themselves and meet their pew mates.

Parish Picnics
Parishioners love events that are not fundraisers—just simple, low-key, fun times together with friends. You might call them "fun-raisers." No agenda. No appeals for money. No massive preparations. No need to go to a distant or fancy place. Like a picnic in the park. Reserve a meadow or pavilion through your community's park office. Or does your parish have enough property with a field or grassy area so you can hold it right there? Just good food, and lots of it. Potluck is great. Or, the parish provides the hot dogs and drinks and parishioners bring the side dishes and desserts. Beer? Maybe yes, maybe no; nothing stronger. Softball, horseshoes (or bocce or whatever the ethnicity of the parish calls for), sack races, perhaps music. Fun for the kids, social time for adults. Have name

tags so everyone can easily learn the names of their fellow parishioners. No charge, or maybe a couple of bucks per head to pay for the meat. A picnic like this is a great opportunity to see the parish as a great big family. Perhaps in June, not deep into the summer when many families are away. Make it an annual event. People will look forward to it and return each year.

Invite everyone as broadly as possible: through the bulletin, pulpit announcements, e-mails, and, always, through telephone and personal contact.

The pastor, all staff and all ministry leaders should be there *to listen*. Parishioners frequently want the pastor's ear to share a thought or a complaint (or even a compliment!). By extension, all parish leaders should be open to the same thing. Picnics are great for this.

Simple Soup

One parish holds occasional, very simple shared meals for interested parishioners, called "Simple Soup. " They are by definition and expectation low-key events with no agenda other than shared time together with friends. Sometimes, a fifteen- to twenty-minute DVD presentation on a pastoral theme might be offered for enrichment.

■ Welcoming New Parishioners

How do you welcome newcomers? Is there anything more than a request to use offertory envelopes?

Does every Sunday bulletin include a box to register as a new parishioner? What kind of follow-up occurs?

Do you offer an after-Mass, outside-the-church opportunity to register even once a year? How about quarterly? Ministry leaders should be right there to talk about different opportunities. Since most people will be eager to be on their way, provide a basic new parishioner package to them and offer to reach them by telephone to continue the conversation.

Do you subscribe to a commercial service that provides names and addresses of new arrivals in the parish neighborhoods? Check with your parish office, where fax ads for these services appear regularly.

How about a parish-based "Welcome Wagon" or "Newcomers" program where each new family would be visited to meet and answer questions? In the ideal world, the pastor would visit the family in their home, but the realities of reduced numbers of priests and the growing list of other duties might make that impossible. The visit could be made by the parochial vicar (if you have one), the deacon, pastoral associate, or members of the welcoming committee. Who visits them is not nearly as important as the fact that someone does! Present a more detailed new family package, perhaps customized to their needs based upon information gleaned from their registration form. The point of the visit is not to find out what the family can do for the parish, but what the parish can do for them. Do they have teens? Are they looking at the parish school for their kids? Do they know about the parish evangelization retreats? Have a brochure about the one coming up. After learning about their interests, they could be invited to participate in appropriate ministries and programs. No commitments necessary, just sharing of information. A friendly visit to welcome them, neighbor to neighbor, with a basket of goodies that includes all the following:

1. A personalized welcome letter, *individually* signed by the pastor. Such letters should *never* begin "Dear New Parishioners." Using the computer's "mail merge" function, information provided by their parish registration should easily allow their name to be included. Different versions of this letter could easily be customized for married couples, couples with schoolchildren, single young adults, seniors, or other sub-sets unique to your parish.

2. The parish mission statement.

3. Basics like Mass schedule, staff lists with titles or roles, telephone numbers and e-mail addresses, Web site address, a map of the parish plant with meeting locations, and room titles.

4. The most recent Sunday bulletin.

5. Brochures or flyers about any upcoming parish events or programs.

6. Listings of all services provided by the parish.

7. Listings of all organizations, including meeting time and location and leader name and telephone number.

8. The parish history.

9. Full information about the parish school (if there is one), including inquiry and registration information.

10. An information flyer and enrollment form for electronic giving.

11. Discount coupons from merchants who are members of the parish, soliciting the newcomers' business.

By the way, Welcome Wagon is a national organization that has been around for almost eighty years. Nearly everyone has heard of it. If it is active in your community, make sure it includes information about your parish.

■ Dinner for New Parishioners

Perhaps quarterly, or as often as needed to keep the group small, the parish should host a dinner for new parish families. All clergy, staff members, pastoral council leadership and key ministerial leadership should attend. This can become a great opportunity to meet everyone and to share important information and the mission statement. A short slide show or PowerPoint presentation could be used here. Child care should be provided.

One parish holds these dinners annually—never as potlucks, always as hosted sit-down dinners for honored guests—and they become significant occasions for the pastor and the staff to recognize the importance of new parishioners.

■ Parish Town Hall Meetings

These events offer a larger opportunity to cover issues and challenges facing the parish. They are led by the pastor and other parish leaders. They engage parishioners by inviting their thoughts and ideas on important parish questions. Unlike coffee after Mass, everyone coming to a town hall meeting expects an agenda. They know that the pastor, all the staff, and all lay ministry leaders will be there. They know, perhaps from the Sunday bulletin or from the pulpit, that certain questions will be covered. It might be the parish budget, or potential implementation of a new ministry. They also know that, while the pastor will probably provide some important information for all parishioners, he and the other parish leaders will be listening to all the feedback given by those present.

Well-run town hall meetings begin on time. They never last more than ninety minutes. They always include the wearing of name tags, shared prayer, warm greetings and thanks for being there, and refreshments. They will probably also have child care provided in an adjoining room by responsible parishioners so parents with families can participate without paying for babysitters.

■ The Annual Parish Town Hall Meeting

A special annual meeting should be led by the pastoral council in the spring, when preparing for the Annual Planning Retreat and before determining budgets. The entire parish community should be invited.

Each person attending should receive the Annual Financial Report and an Annual Ministry Report that includes an update on all ministries and a review of accomplishments shown against last year's statement of goals and objectives. The program should also include recognition of all lay ministers.

The chairperson of the pastoral council should lead a discussion seeking input from everyone on these five major areas. Modify this list as needed.

1. What are the parish's strengths?

2. What are its areas of concern?

3. What do you wish the parish would do more of? Less of?

4. How effective is a particular ministry?

5. What are your hopes and dreams for the parish?

6. If money were no object, what ministries would you add to the parish?

▪ Listening Meetings

Listening meetings differ from town hall meetings because they are not led by anyone from parish leadership, and thus provide the best possible opportunity to hear what parishioners are really thinking and feeling. They must be carefully planned, from the invitation to the post-meeting processing of the results, for everyone to know that they are "for real." We are all surrounded by so much noise in our lives, every second of every day, that the very notion of being listened to doesn't immediately make sense. If Father announces from the pulpit that he is scheduling listening meetings, most people probably won't take it seriously, suspecting that what he really wants is to talk to them (or at them), almost certainly for the purpose of asking for more money. That's why it is so important to treat the invitation to such an event seriously.

Create your listening meetings with these characteristics.

- Father should not be the one to lead the discussions. After an introductory welcome and prayer, he (and any other staff there) should leave. Bring in a neutral facilitator and recorder so that all ideas, comments, and concerns can be freely given and anonymously recorded. At the same time, anyone expressing a very strong opinion should be asked whether they are giving permission for someone to contact them to become more involved.

- They begin and end on time, lasting only one hour.

- They have a clear agenda, with focus questions that will generate rich data, as well as leaving participants with feelings that attending the meeting was worthwhile.

- Think out carefully just what questions you want answers to. Get input from different segments of pastoral leadership before making this decision. Be specific. Limit an individual session to just a very few particular topics. Pick questions that will generate answers that parish leaders can use.

- Schedule listening meetings sparingly, no more than twice a year. Use each one for important feedback so parishioners will learn that it is worth their time to participate.

- Think quality feedback, not quantity. Don't aim for hundreds to attend each session. Invite enough different people so that twenty show up for each one, but hold enough different sessions that many people have opportunities to attend. That way, all present will have opportunities to share their views and won't get lost in the crowd.

- Select those to be invited from many different parts of the parish: Mass-goers, school parents, school alumni, ministry leaders. Perhaps Father should make some calls to inactive parishioners and invite their ideas. The point is to hear many different points of view, not just the opinions of those who are good friends of the pastor. Remember to pick enough names at random to allow for those who will decline the invitation.

• The pastor himself should do the inviting in personal letters. Assure each person that this is an invitation to attend a single one-hour meeting—no one is being asked to serve on an ongoing committee. Following the letter of invitation, a team of parish leaders should reach each person by telephone to confirm their willingness to participate and to choose a particular meeting.

• Schedule them in clusters, offering different sessions on different days and at different times during a seven-day period so that each person can choose one that works: perhaps a Tuesday evening at 6 PM and 7:30 PM, a Thursday at 10 AM and 2 PM, a Saturday afternoon at 1 PM and again ninety minutes before the Vigil Mass, and a Sunday morning after each of two different Masses. This is merely a suggestion. The point is to reach the many different people of your parish with their many different schedules.

• Assure everyone who attends that their opinions will make a difference. Promise to provide each person with a summary of the discussion within ten days and follow that with another update in six months describing what changed in the parish because of their opinions.

• Then, stick to your promises.

■ The "Time and Talent" Part of Stewardship

Seeking Information

Each time a parish minister reaches a parishioner, it is an opportunity to gather time and talent information. But doing it one parishioner at a time can take a long time. Your parish might want to consider a more organized ways to get a lot of information about many different people.

- Make sure that the new parishioner welcome process includes opportunities to learn this information about each member of the family.

- Hold a "Time and Talent" Sunday and invite each person at Mass to complete a pre-printed card distributed (with pencils) by ushers.

- Ask the Telephone Tree Ministers to reach everyone with a pre-scripted survey. Be sure to give everyone specific training ahead of time.

- Always have "Time and Talent" survey forms available in the parish office. Each time someone comes in for a pastoral appointment, invite them to complete the survey while waiting.

Putting Information to Use

Most parish management software programs have convenient ways to record information learned about individual members. It might be listed as "gifts" or "talents" or "interests" or "professional expertise" or even "hobbies."

Whatever it's called, the important point is to learn to use this part of the software program. Every time some new information is learned, whether via a one-on-one or through a more organized approach, it should be recorded in the parish database, making this a richer and richer information investment as time goes by. At the beginning, though, it is extremely important to learn how your program works. To assure consistency and an easy ability to extract worthwhile information, it may be necessary to create a list of "key words," essentially a standardized list of possible entries that might match all the possible jobs which you could anticipate needing.

Otherwise, be mindful of the old computer expression, "Garbage in, garbage out." For example, if you enter "great cook" and someone else uses "culinary skills," you will never find one another's entries.

Once your database has a useful amount of talent information, learn how to use it to match a need with a person. After all, doesn't it make sense to invite people to do what they do best or what they enjoy doing?

What the Pastor Can Do

One of the terms found later in this book in the chapter on the planning process is that of "lead agent." The pastor should be the lead agent in making certain that the parish is a welcoming and hospitable one in every way. He alone in his role as parish leader can model the very behavior he expects of all other staff and lay ministry leaders and constantly monitor all parish activity to see that this same style is found in all aspects of parish life. He is in a unique position to see that any parochial vicar assigned to the parish shares a sense of the importance of these qualities.

At each weekend Mass, the pastor or other priest should welcome and introduce all new families during his announcements. He can also make a general statement of welcome to all visitors.

Perhaps once a month, at the time when other announcements are being made, the priest can invite parishioners to get up and share their own news, perhaps about new babies, anniversaries with zeroes on the end, and the like. Everyone loves good news.

The priest celebrant should be present outside the front doors of the church before and after each Sunday Mass to visit with parishioners.

The pastor should personally contact each newly registered family within ten days, after Mass on Sunday or by telephone. How extraordinary for a new family to receive a personal telephone call from the pastor! Admittedly, in an era of shrinking numbers of priests, this duty might be given to a Welcome Committee. The important value here is the welcoming call itself, from whomever it comes.

The pastor can hold regular monthly Sunday morning breakfasts and evening dinners around the rectory table with small groups of parishioners, perhaps those who have been identified for potential ministerial roles. This forum gives him an opportunity to get acquainted with them and to listen to their hopes and dreams for the parish.

What Parochial Vicars, Deacons, and Other Staff Can Do

Other priests and deacons have roles similar to the pastor in that they lead liturgical events in ways that laypeople don't. Like the pastor, they can meet and greet parishioners in front of the church before and after Masses.

Priests can assist the pastor in telephoning or visiting new parishioners soon after they arrive in the parish.

All staff members, lay or ordained, are representatives of the parish. The pastor can't be everywhere. They should be present at all gatherings and events to welcome and greet parishioners. In their roles as planners and coordinators, they have the additional opportunity to see that these qualities are built into all such events.

Staff members should make certain that all new members are appropriately welcomed, since the pastor might not be aware of the arrival of every new person.

What Lay Ministry Leaders Can Do

As leaders of individual ministries, these laypeople should model welcoming and hospitality within their own groups. They are on the front line and can make certain that all their members feel included.

Likewise, they can best make training and formation needs known to the pastor, the staff, or the pastoral council. They perhaps know these needs better than anyone.

What the Pastoral Council Can Do

The pastoral council, in its oversight role, should monitor both the development and the implementation of processes for welcoming and hospitality. This is a never-ending role and should not be relegated to a once-a-year task. Since council members are most likely to be present for many events and services, they have a unique role in ensuring that these values are lived out every day.

What Liturgical Ministers (Greeters and Ushers) Can Do

Since greeters and ushers are, like the parish secretary, on the front line and may be the first contact that visitors have with the parish, they must be helped to see themselves as representatives of the church. They more than anyone can assure that parishioners and guests are welcomed warmly at Mass on Sunday.

Because most greeters and ushers serve at the same Mass each week, they know who the regulars are. They can quickly spot when one is missing, perhaps because of illness, and can alert appropriate parish staff. Conversely, they know new faces when they see them and can introduce themselves and welcome those who are considering joining the parish. Greeters and ushers should be provided with an easy way to alert others in charge of hospitality of such newcomers.

Whether we simply want to make the parish a better place or we are planning a major capital drive, it is the duty of ministry leaders to provide the opportunities for parishioners, both active and inactive, to be heard. People flourish with personal attention—authentic personal attention, not something that is mass-produced to look like it's personal.

Listening leads to inviting. Inviting leads to involving. (Refer back to Chapter 7.)

THE BIG QUESTIONS

Father Dan O'Hanlon was a theologian and ecumenical leader who taught at the Jesuit School of Theology at Berkeley, California, prior to his death in 1992. He wrote that "the most relevant thing the Church can do, by preaching the gospel and celebrating the Lord's Supper, is to equip men and women with the courage and compassion they need to serve the world. Obviously, if this is done in a slovenly, half-hearted way, it can be dreadfully irrelevant, and can confirm nominal Christians in their isolation from the problems of their brothers [and sisters]. But if it is done in such a way as to make the Risen Lord vividly present among us, it can give us what we all desperately need: faith, hope and love" (*National Catholic Reporter*, October 8, 1971).

If your pastoral council were to use this quote as a mission statement, how would your parish be a different place?

BIBLIOGRAPHY AND ASSOCIATED RESOURCES

For nearly eighty years, Welcome Wagon has specialized in offering free gifts to newly arrived residents in most U.S. cities. Their gift baskets usually feature special offers, coupons, and savings from local merchants. Go to www.welcomewagon.com to learn how your parish package for new members can be included.

There was a time when Newcomers' Club offered some competition to Welcome Wagon. In recent years, however, Newcomers' Club has become a singles-meeting-singles group for those newly arrived, whereas Welcome Wagon has held on to its traditional role.

The Institute of School and Parish Development (www.ispd.com), referenced frequently throughout this book, offers good materials on listening meetings. Look at their resource paper titled "Input Sessions and Their Value" for starters.

CHAPTER 15

"What We Have Here Is a Failure to Communicate!"

But you will receive power when the Holy Spirit has come upon you; and you will be my witnesses in Jerusalem, in all Judea and Samaria, and to the ends of the earth.

Acts 1:8

■ A Personal Story

One year in January, I received two different envelopes in the mail from my parish. Each contained a form letter. Neither was personalized, each was written to "Dear Parishioner." One thanked me for my work during the previous year with "the youth group." (A blank had been filled in.) The other complained that my offertory gifts didn't seem to come up to the pastor's expectations, considering his perception of my income level. Another filled-in blank listed the amount he thought I should be giving. Both were mimeographed.

■ What is wrong with this picture?

New Words—New Thinking

Advertising agencies approach client campaigns in two different ways: "frequency" and "reach." "Frequency" means how many times each person is touched by a message. "Reach" means how many people you can touch in a given area or market. Good advertising campaigns always aim for a frequency of at least three. They claim that the reach is not nearly as important as a minimum frequency of three. In other words, no matter how many people you send messages to, each person who received the message has to receive it at least three times to be effective. Strictly speaking, frequency is much more important than reach. (How many times did you see that noisy "Sham-wow" commercial before you succumbed?)

Can this be true? Have we become so desensitized that we must be nearly hit over the head for something to register? The answer appears to be "Yes." After all, we are deluged with information. We get so many e-mails that we are forced to rely on filters provided by the carrier to screen out the majority of them. The number of TV commercials has grown so much that it's easy to take five-minute breaks when they start. I recently completely microwaved a frozen meal during one commercial break. (Remember when there was only one commercial at a time?) If we go to the movie and arrive early, we must endure several minutes of advertising slides, *most of which repeat at least three times*, and other commercials before the film begins.

Let's translate this idea into church terms for a moment. We put an announcement in the parish bulletin only to find it completely ignored. We tell everyone that an event deadline for registration exists and yet no one signs up on time. We send costly letters to parishioners asking for help with the religious education program, yet no one calls. What is the problem here? Why are our parishioners inattentive or unresponsive to our messages? We would like to believe that everyone on the mailing list is as interested in the parish as we are. Yet, they don't seem to pay attention to what we are telling them. Perhaps the problem is that we haven't thought about this "rule of threes."

One reason for this seeming lack of interest is the perception that every time the parish contacts them, they are being asked for something (usually money!). This is, after all, not entirely an incorrect perception. Another is that the e-mail message from the church, if not immediately answered, slips farther and farther down the list in the Inbox and becomes so old that it is gradually relegated to Trash. Hasn't that happened to each of us? You receive a letter or an e-mail message that seems very interesting. You want to answer it but not right now. You just don't have time. You'll get to it. But then twenty-five more e-mails take precedence. That once important message slips way down the list. A deadline passes. "Oh, well." But what if you read about it in the bulletin, you heard about it in a pulpit announcement, and you got an e-mail about it?

Perhaps we need to think in the same terms: *more attention to "frequency."* (How much attention we give to "reach" is a different matter and may have to do with the sizes of our active and inactive lists.) Perhaps the lesson here is that **effective communications with parishioners is built upon multiple messages on the same subject.** Is it any wonder why the annual Christmas appeal to inactive parishioners generates so little response? Is that appeal letter the only time they hear from us all year? Keep this new rule, the "Rule of Threes," in your mind as you examine the communication suggestions offered in this chapter.

■ In-Person Communications

Parish Office Encounters

We've discussed various aspects of office staff encounters in other chapters. The only issue remaining is to make certain that all office staff members are fully "on board" regarding anything anyone might come in to talk or ask about. Don't leave the receptionists or telephone staff or secretaries out of the loop on upcoming events or recent changes in parish policy or practices.

Greeters in Front of Church

Seek greeters from all the ethnic and age groups. Cover all the entrances, not just the front doors. Remind them to remember badges and smiles.

The Parish Telephone Tree

When you need to get the word out, short of an in-person visit, nothing works better than a telephone call. You can use bulletin articles, pulpit announcements, flyers under the wiper blade of every car in the parking lot, and e-mail messages, but a telephone call is better than any of these. Obviously, though, it doesn't happen without a lot of organization and work.

Here's how to get it done.

1. First and foremost, treat it as a ministry. It's part of the communication and outreach ministry of the parish. It's not just a grungy job. Invite and prepare a specific group of parishioners, some of whom are available during the day and others who are available in the evenings. During their preparatory program, stress the ministerial nature of their work. Then, give them hands-on training on telephone techniques. Include some role-playing opportunities to prepare them for the many different responses they will receive.

2. Give each member of the tree fifteen names and numbers. You might ask each one to first select five to seven parishioners whom they already know and to pick the remainder from the general list.

3. Appoint a chairperson, who can be called when the tree needs to be activated.

4. Use the tree to invite members to parish functions, like an annual picnic, or to make them aware of the Holy Week schedule. Use it to communicate an important message from the pastor. Use it selectively to reach parishioners who

haven't been seen in the parish for a while. Use it judicious-
ly, however, so the Telephone Tree Ministers don't get burnt
out. Give them a time frame for completing their calls.

5. During each telephone call, they should be instructed to ask
the parish member if they want to be called in the future
about church events and what time of day or evening is best
to reach them. Some parishioners might also indicate that
they prefer e-mail notification. Be sure to accurately record
their e-mail address. Always end the call with a "thank
you."

6. Provide a convenient way for them to report their results
when they are finished.

■ Other Communications—Staying in Touch with Registered Parishioners

Parish Member Information

Rigorously keep your parish database up to date. Good, Catholic-
based church management software packages offer opportunities
for so much more than addresses and donation records. If you
are just beginning, do a Google search for "church management
software" to identify several different products. Perhaps more important, talk to neighboring parishes or the diocesan office to see
what programs seem best. All these programs can list members of a
family, preferred primary language, and birthdays. Individuals can
be flagged for leadership involvement, ministry interest, council
or committee membership, Sacramental history, and much more.
Using such software, it would, for instance, be so easy to send personalized letters to all pastoral council members with a meeting reminder, or to send each parishioner a birthday card. Have you ever
received a birthday card from your parish? (This is covered in more
detail a little later in this chapter.)

These software packages usually include appropriate salutation information ("Dear Mr. and Mrs. Johnson," "Dear Sally," etc., or similar salutations in Spanish, for instance) for "mail merge" letters. It is not necessary to ever send out a "Dear Parishioner" letter ever again.

"Mail merge" is a computer term describing the process where customized salutation information, for instance, is merged into letters where the body of the letter remains the same. Another use of a merge letter is including member-specific donation information into an otherwise identical letter format. Identical letters in appropriate languages, using the computer's knowledge of each family's preferred primary language could easily be constructed.

"GIGO," another computer expression, is an acronym for "Garbage in, garbage out". Simply put, the only way to get good information out of a computer program like that described above is to put good information in, with an investment of time to keep your database current and accurate. How annoying and upsetting it is to a widow to continue to receive mailings from her parish still addressed to her deceased husband, who was probably buried from that very parish, simply because no one on the staff has linked information in the death register to the parish database. Of course, this requires properly trained staff who enter correct information in for each family. The value of such a well-kept database is cumulative. That is, as time goes by, and the database is made more and more accurate, its value increases accordingly.

Birthday Cards

Each month, print a list of upcoming birthdays from the parish database. The Birthday Committee gathers to hand-address all envelopes. Use real birthday cards. Companies that supply parishes with bereavement or Mass intention cards can probably supply church-oriented birthday cards, too. Each committee member personalizes the cards to parishioners personally known. Pastoral council members can do the same at each monthly meeting. The cards are then placed in a prominent place in the office so that staff members and other ministers can scan the cards to offer personal greetings as they go by.

Other Ministries of Greeting

Following the approach with birthday cards, similar committees can be formed to send personal messages to shut-ins, those who have recently experienced deaths in the family, and the elderly. Marriage Encounter folks could be enlisted to do the same for wedding anniversaries of parishioners.

Your Sunday Bulletin

Visit several neighboring parishes and compare your bulletin to theirs. How does yours look? Is it attractive to the eye? Is it easy to find important information? Is it accurate? Are there any typographical errors? Then, look at the last ten bulletins from your parish. Is there an appropriate consistency of design that allows the reader to quickly find a certain kind of information? That is, is the Mass schedule always on the same page? Or the reflections on the readings? Or the staff telephone list?

Are some items repeated, week after week, so that the reader begins to wonder if the bulletin contains anything new? At the same time, is there variety, perhaps of cover graphic or ink color, or content, that makes it fresh each week? Is the typeface easy to read? Is the printing process used to duplicate your bulletin one of quality so that the parishioner with poor eyesight can still read it? Locate a subscription service that provides a steady stream of seasonal graphics for bulletin use. These companies frequently offer bulletin layout advice as well. Does your bulletin need to be bilingual? Don't try to answer that question yourself. Go to parishioners for whom English is their second language and ask them. Warning: It is no small task to regularly produce a totally bilingual weekly bulletin.

Your Parish Web site

Is the parish Web site address prominently displayed in every Sunday bulletin? Enlist the aid of a tech-savvy parish high school student to make and keep your Web site attractive and interesting. You will probably have two costs.

First, there may be a charge for a Web site template. Commercial Web site development sites offer great templates so you don't have to create an attractive one from scratch. Just Google for "church Web site templates" or, better yet, "free church Web site templates." A brief search will uncover lots of templates, some of which are free. Others don't cost much to download, and then you will be on your way! Pick one that will be attractive to your parishioners and personalize it with your own parish information. Don't minimize the importance of this design decision. Just as the appearance of your parish property is important to create a good first impression, so is the appearance of the home page of your Web site. If it's uninteresting or too complicated and cluttered, the visitor will be turned off and go no further.

Second, you will need to pay a small monthly or quarterly fee to a Web site hosting service. This is the company that actually has your Web site pages on its computers. There are two values here. First, you don't need to keep one dedicated computer running around the clock for potential Web site visitors. Second, no one can "hack" into your computer and steal or corrupt valuable information, because the Web site isn't actually on your computer. Again, do a "Google" search for "Web site hosting." If you have a computer professional in your parish, that person can help narrow the field for you so you don't drown in techno-babble or aren't overwhelmed with choices.

Here are some other suggestions. Ask the designer of your Web site to create all the pages as editable templates, so that each staff member can regularly review certain pages to keep them accurate. In other words, all the formatting should be built in so that staff can come in and merely change the text without disturbing the "look" of the page. Don't get caught in the bind where you must pay your consultant for weekly updating. Also, if you haven't made any edits in three months, then it is probably not relevant to parishioners. Keep your Web site simple and straightforward so that visitors can actually find what they came there for. Do this by providing a "Site Map" button on your home page, allowing a user to find any page quickly. Also, don't make the site so "deep," meaning that a user must click from one page to another and another to find information, or some pages will never be discovered. Last, keep a counter on the home page so you know how many hits it is receiving. (Your resident techno-geek will know how to do that.)

Once your site is up, keep it current. Always include the following:

- On the first page (called the "home page"), list all the basics: the Mass schedule, telephone numbers, directions to the parish, staff names and titles. A box with the times of Masses is extremely important if an upcoming holy day or holiday has any departure from the known schedule, like Thanksgiving Day. But strike a balance here. All this information is very important, but so is a manageable home page. If it's visually too much for one page, have easy links right there. A link is a button that takes you to another page with the desired information.

- Is there a page with each staff member's e-mail address? Set it up so that a click on the e-mail address takes the user directly to an e-mail message screen.

- Does the Web site always include this week's bulletin?

- If the pastor prepares his weekly homily in writing, it could easily be included along with references to the liturgical theme and Scripture readings of the day.

- Is there a timely or seasonal message from the pastor? The same letter that the pastor sends to all members at Christmas can easily appear on your Web site.

- Do the pastoral council and finance council maintain pages with minutes of their most recent meetings, any appropriate reports, and announcements about their next meetings? Listings of members of these two very important groups and their e-mail addresses should also be available.

- The main reason that people will come to the parish Web site is to learn about forthcoming events. Is there a page of "Announcements" or "Upcoming Events" with fresh and timely news about parish life? Include a calendar showing all parish activities, times, and locations. *Keep it updated!* One click of a button from the home page should take you to this page.

- It's easy to have sign-up sheets for religious education or sacramental preparation programs that can be filled in online and sent directly to the parish with a click of a button.

- Is there a page where the visitor can request more information, a "Contact us" page? Ask visitors if they would like to receive regular e-mails about parish programs. This can even be subdivided into various categories, like prayer groups, youth ministry, or religious education. Using your browser's "Categories" function, it's easy to put e-mail addresses into as many different groupings as you need.

- Can a visitor register as a parishioner from the Web site?

- Can a visitor sign up for timely e-mail messages from the parish with information about current events, or special Mass schedules for a holy day?

- Is there a page with links to your diocesan Web site? The U.S. Catholic Conference Web site? The Vatican Web site? Other

Catholic Web sites? Check out other parish and diocesan Web sites for ideas for these links.

After the parish Web site is up, reliable and current, it's time to consider more sophisticated additions.

- Streaming video from inside the church. Streaming video means live video (like TV) in almost real time. Any high-speed PC would be capable of receiving streaming video. Offer webcasts of Sunday Masses, perhaps daily Masses, and special events like First Communion or confirmation. One very international parish announced that the First Communion Mass would be the first to be webcast. E-mail messages immediately went around the world to family members, and that Mass had viewers from all across the Philippine Islands and many other Pacific Rim countries!

- Archived video of the pastor's last five Sunday homilies. They could easily be made available for download as podcast audio files as well.

- Archived video of a group of parishioners praying the rosary—all five decades, a different video for each of the mysteries. This could be of great assistance for infirm parishioners to keep a prayer life at home.

- Archived video of parish events, such as the St. Patrick's Day dinner-dance, or the eighth-grade championship basketball game, could also be available with the click of a button. In one parish, the high school youth group has taken on the ministry of operating the cameras and technical equipment to broadcast these events. After all, young people are very adept at these tasks.

- Provide a page for members (or guests) to make contributions or payments for programs, like religious education classes. Chapter 6 includes a discussion on the appropriateness of electronic giving. Your parish leaders should come to an agreement on that issue before moving forward. If you agree to do it, then one method not discussed in that chapter is the opportunity to contribute via your Web site. Two options are immediately apparent. One way is a page where a donor fills in the fields for a credit card transaction (card number, expiration date, etc.—you know the drill). Before beginning this, check with your credit card merchant service to make certain you get everything you need. At the click of a button, the completed page is sent to the church office as an e-mail message, where the transaction is completed using the parish's credit card terminal. It is possible to connect this page directly to your credit card provider, making the transaction instantaneous, but that might be for later. The other method is a payment through an online company that provides payment services, like Paypal (www.paypal.com). Users of these services on both ends of the transaction know that they are fully protected from fraud. All that is needed is that the parish become a member of the service, which allows it to receive payments. This is a very user-friendly approach, for both the parish and the donor.

- Customized pages for special groups, like the pastoral council, Small Christian Communities, or unusually active parish organizations so that they can communicate with one another.

- A blog page for the pastor. "Blog" is a contraction of "Web log" and is an easy way for someone on staff, like the pastor or the youth minister, to post comments and for visitors to chat online with that person. It functions in real time and makes computer interaction much more personal. A pastor blog would make it easy for him to share some of his daily pastoral activities and for visitors to react, or to invite feedback about last Saturday's fundraising dinner.

Churches with very active and complex Web sites know that it is difficult, if not impossible, to keep them totally up to date and free of errors. Naturally, the computer industry has developed software to solve that problem! Content management systems software (CMS) keeps pages accurate by using templates for the page design and databases for changeable information. To accomplish this, CMS packages merge the two. For instance, if the religious education office were to get a new telephone number, one entry in the CMS software would change it everywhere it appeared on the Web site. These packages even use expiration dates to control when certain pages come online and are later removed (like the Holy Week schedule). As usual, a Google search will lead you to appropriate vendors.

There is really no limit to the types of communications that can be done on the Web. For example, I recently attended a virtual (online) trade show for photographers. The home page began with a ticket booth, where the visitor registered with an e-mail address, then moved to a picture of the entrance lobby to this type of event, with different doors for a resource center (with links to various online services), the auditorium (where workshops were offered), the exhibit hall (for vendor booths), and the networking café (to chat with others on the subject). Simply clicking on each door took the user to that location. How easily this concept could be used for a parish *Ministry Fair*! Of course, this would take good technical proficiency to create, but it is well within the skill set of an experienced Web site administrator. Keep an open mind to other Web uses that you see, check out other really good church sites, and use your imagination!

Using E-mail

With apologies to the U.S. Postal Service, e-mail is rapidly replacing snail mail as the best way to reach people. It is certainly the fastest! Get e-mail addresses from parishioners and use e-mail, perhaps once a month, with ultra-current information, like deadlines and upcoming events. Will a special Mass be offered on Thanksgiving Day at a time different from the regular daily Mass schedule? Or will annual offering tax letters be sent to everyone this week? Tell everyone in an e-mail message.

Yes, e-mail addresses change a lot, and, yes. they need a lot of maintaining, but the tradeoff is that e-mailings cost nothing. With postage approaching fifty cents per letter, not to mention paper, envelopes, printing costs, and staff assembly time, the investment in maintaining a current e-mail list is well worth it. How difficult would it be to place the following boxed item in this Sunday's bulletin?

Did you receive e-mail from the parish last week?

E-mail news from St. Brunhilde's was sent last Tuesday. Did you receive yours? Do we have a current e-mail address for your family? Simply provide yours in the box at the bottom of this page. By the way, make sure that your spam filter allows our message in by including info@stbrunhilde.com in your e-mail program. And remember: We will never give your e-mail address to anyone.

By the way, don't use e-mail just to ask for money! Think about sending e-mailings every month about parish news and events. Start by sending a general message about all upcoming events. Later, using the suggestion found in the previous section on Web sites, ask visitors if they would like to receive regular e-mails about specific programs in various categories, like prayer groups, youth ministry, or religious education. These e-mail messages do not need to be complex or lengthy; they need only to provide timely news about a specific area of parish life. Use your browser's "Categories" function to put e-mail addresses into as many different groupings as you need.

Staying in Touch with Inactive Parishioners

Unless someone dies, or moves to Antarctica, or is so angry with your parish or the church that they never want to hear from you again, you should probably not delete them from your database. After all, at one point, they were interested in a connection with your parish. Perhaps a better approach might be to classify different levels of involvement, like these:

1. Registered parishioners using offertory envelopes.

2. Registered parishioners declining envelopes. (This delineation is important so that you can easily send a proper list to your envelope supplier.)

3. Inactive parishioners still residing in the parish.

4. Former parishioners who have moved away but still want to stay in touch.

5. Those who have moved away or have become invisible.

6. You might have other categories that would work better for your needs.

If your particular software program has no provision for classifying family involvement, use different ranges of family account numbers for each of these categories.

Of course, if someone states that they don't want further information from your parish, by letter or e-mail, you should respect their wishes. In fact, some states have laws requiring you to remove a name from your e-mail list if the person requests that you do so.

Different mailings and e-mailings can be addressed to each group. Just remember: in *no* case should the only mailing of the year to anyone be an annual Christmas appeal for a donation. Remember, too, that even those who have moved away (Group 4 in the list above) may still hold a warm feeling for the old parish and appreciate occasional news from it.

■ Other Paper Mailings

Yes, there is still a place for paper mailings, which are actually hand-carried by a letter carrier and put into the mailboxes of your parishioners. This is still necessary for annual parish offertory envelopes, tickets for raffles, Christmas calendars, and the like. Remember the birthday card suggested above? Further, the reality will probably always be that some parishioners will not have e-mail accounts. Additionally, with paper mail, you have the opportunity to reach everyone, including those who do not attend Mass and take a Sunday bulletin. If you reduce the number of paper mailings by using e-mail more often, then the occasional paper mailing will perhaps take on more importance to the recipient. This means that you should plan more carefully just which items will go through the mail.

THE BIG QUESTIONS

How many of your Sunday assembly are registered parishioners? Do you know? How can you find out?

Can you identify a parishioner in the communications or advertising field with a strong personal faith who might be able to help translate concepts from their work into ideas with ministerial usefulness?

Can you identify a tech-savvy parishioner who can become your webmaster (your Web site lead agent)? That person needs Web site and Web page management skills and can take responsibility for keeping yours completely current and accurate.

Equally important is the person who manages your e-mail address database. E-mail addresses change much more frequently than street addresses. Preserve the investment you have made in accurate listings by faithfully recording all changes and additions.

BIBLIOGRAPHY AND ASSOCIATED RESOURCES

Church management software falls into the computer category known as "industry-specific" software. That is, it is written for a narrow, specific audience and not for the broad, general public, like a word processor, for instance. The consequence is that industry-specific packages are usually expensive. The value comes from the fact that they perform very specific tasks for a parish in ways that more general software cannot. Look specifically for packages aimed at Catholic parishes. They "speak our language" and address uniquely Catholic issues, like sacramental history of members.

One well-known package is the Parish Data System. Check out www.parishdata.com for details.

Whichever package you choose, invest the extra dollars in training for your staff so that you can squeeze from it every benefit and feature that the software offers. Think about benefits like birthdays, identifying ministries and talents, etc. Talk to your diocesan pastoral ministry offices for critiques of these packages.

Paypal (www.paypal.com) is perhaps the best known online payment service. It is completely reliable and is used in nearly every area of Internet commerce. Any parishioner doing business on the Internet will be familiar with Paypal, which will increase the ready acceptance of such a service.

CHAPTER 16

Inviting the Un-Churched In
Outreach

And this good news of the kingdom will be proclaimed throughout the world, as a testimony to all the nations; and then the end will come.

Matthew 24:14

Catholics have never been very good at outreach. A cynic might say that Catholics have a certain smugness from the belief that we belong to the one true church. Because Catholic churches were once so full, with a richness of parish life, most members probably never felt any need to look for converts. The occasional convert that came in as a result of a mixed marriage was good enough. After all, the number of Catholic babies baptized into the church seemed to keep the rolls replenished.

Things have changed. Demographics have changed. Old-time Catholic populations have died off. Aggressive evangelization efforts by the Mormons, Seventh-day Adventists, Jehovah's Witnesses and various Protestant churches have clearly cut into formerly "safe" Catholic areas in many cities. While many immigrant groups, like Mexicans, Latin Americans, and Filipinos are predominantly Catholic, the way they live out their faith life is in some ways so different that traditional born-in-the-USA Catholics have great difficulty accepting them into their parishes, or re-inventing their parishes to be more inclusive. Recent priest scandals have nudged many Catholics away into other denominations, or toward a purely personal "Me and God" belief. Numbers of priests are shrinking. Dioceses around the country must make hard choices to close or consolidate many parishes, much to the dismay of old-time Catholics. The church just isn't the same.

The concept of evangelization of baptized Catholics was covered in Chapter 3. In Chapter 14, we explored reaching into our parish to meet everyone already identified as Catholic. Here, the topic is extended to invite in those outside the church. The ministry of outreach is uncharted waters for many Catholics and many parishes.

■ A Definition of Terms

Catholic outreach can cover several different areas:

1. **Non-Catholics who live within the parish boundaries.** A Christian non-Catholic looking for a church to join would probably not usually look to a Catholic parish but would instead look to other churches in the community of one's own denomination or a similarly disposed denomination. Reaching non-Catholics would take serious outreach effort, like door-to-door canvassing.

2. **Catholics in other parishes.** Because of the territorial nature of Catholic parishes, most pastors would probably not engage in efforts to encourage them to move.

3. **Invisible members of the parish.** This area of outreach was covered in Chapter 14.

4. **This leaves visitors to your parish.** This chapter will limit itself to consideration of those who come to the parish as visitors—for a wedding, a funeral, as guests of parishioners on Sunday morning, or who may be looking for a worship community to join.

■ Some Principles of Catholic Outreach

- Know what your parish stands for. Internalize your parish's mission statement. Know why you are inviting someone to join your church. It can't be just to increase numbers.

- Evangelization must be a priority for the entire parish, not just you, for it to succeed. When a new face appears at Sunday Mass, that person must feel a sense of welcome from everyone there, not just you. Acknowledge and recognize visitors at every Mass.

- Members of your parish must know why they are Catholic and be willing to share that conviction with others. Lukewarm Catholics will never inspire others to join. The Catholic Church is sacrament-based, which is not true for every Protestant denomination, and members need to have *celebrated* the sacraments in their own lives. Do most Catholics understand that sacraments are the celebration of God's presence in the midst of their community at moments of great human experience; like marriage, the moment of solemn commitment between two particular members, or the entrance of a new member into the community in baptism, or the moment of reconciliation with our neighbor, or the joy of making an adult commitment to the faith in confirmation, or preparing the community for the movement of a gravely ill member from the church on earth to the church in heaven in the sacrament of the sick, or the daily remembrance of who we are as Catholics in the Eucharist? If

Catholics never experienced celebration at these moments, or if Catholics don't see sacraments celebrated that way for others, neither will potential new Catholics.

- Make sure that the "pro" of Catholic social teachings isn't drowned out by the "anti." Does everyone understand, for instance, that the church takes a strong stand in favor of all life—that it isn't only anti-abortion—that it equally opposes capital punishment and unjust war?

- Offer regular, well-publicized opportunities for non-Catholics to learn about the church, inquiry classes, if you will. The RCIA offers that to those who have committed to enter the church, but something less formal is needed as a first step.

- Another chapter of this book described great parishes as places where it's easy to be good. Make certain that your parish lives out the values it proclaims. As important as welcoming receptionists and friendly sacristans are to existing members, they are perhaps even more important to the non-parishioner who has an encounter with a Catholic parish.

- Your ministry of hospitality will help any visitor feel welcome: a warm smile and greeting by someone at the church entrance, a person wearing a greeter badge, properly trained on how to treat visitors and what to say to them. During the week, is the sacristan or the custodian equipped to do this? Can they escort a visitor (escort, not point the way) to the church office or the meeting room they seek?

- Small Christian communities and neighborhood mini-parishes will provide opportunities for meaningful engagement with the church not only for existing members but for those looking at the Catholic church as well. Potential members will be attracted in part by the unique Catholic message but also by the opportunities for prayer and fellowship found so often in these smaller settings.

- Perhaps the pastor should take a walk through the church parking lot during Sunday Masses (preferably when he is not the presider!) to observe the number of husbands reading newspapers and listening to football games in their cars while their wives are in church. Perhaps unchurched husbands should be the first group the parish tries to reach. One study of absentee husbands suggested that men stayed away from Mass because it was boring, dull, and mediocre in its execution, going on to suggest that men would find liturgy done with excellence much more attractive. Of course, excellent liturgy will attract many people, not just absentee husbands, especially if it is indicative of a broader excellence of parish life. The same study suggested that the broad unwillingness of men to admit their weaknesses made the parish Web site an excellent way to reach them. Men can anonymously download homilies or other resources on "guy" topics like "How do I keep my eye on my wife, and not on that attractive woman at work?" or "How can I get more involved in my kids' lives?" or "I need help breaking away from Internet pornography." They may never speak about it, but men will listen to well-done presentations on topics like these; and they may be drawn closer to Jesus Christ as a result.

- One pastor described passing out small slips of paper and asking all in attendance one Sunday to write the names of three non-Catholics they knew and to list their relationships to these names on one side. On the other, he asked them to write the names of three Catholics they know who no longer attended Mass or were otherwise inactive in the church, again with their relationships listed. He was surprised to see how many of these names were those of family members.

He and the parish leadership began to take steps to reach these people to help them connect (or reconnect) with the parish.

- Many years ago, John Quinn, the retired archbishop of San Francisco, spoke at a synod of bishops in Rome. He challenged all priests to become models of Christian joy, complaining that if he were a person outside the church and encountered a grumpy or otherwise joyless priest, it would do nothing to encourage him to become involved. That admonition can easily be extended to all in the church. People are more likely to find personal meaning in a church where they feel welcomed and where members seem to find joy in belonging.

- If bad music, uninspiring homilies, and unkempt churches drive away marginal Catholics, think of the impact upon someone looking for a place to belong.

The most immediate issue might be to examine what happens to a non-Catholic visitor to your church on Sunday morning. Yes, it is possible that your parish might have visitors who are looking for a church to join. Of course, if they choose never to return, then you will probably never know that they were there at all. There are many reasons why they don't ever come back.

- They were not welcomed at the door. No one seemed to notice that they were visitors.

- It was difficult to find a seat because so many people held on to their good seats at the ends of the pews.

- There was no provision for small children or infants during the Mass.

- They were not greeted or welcomed, either by an usher or from the altar.

- They didn't feel a sense of hospitality or warmth once they were in the assembly.

- Everyone seemed to just trudge along during the Mass, without a sense of joy or spirituality.

- The church seemed to have a "members only" feeling, especially in the conversations before Mass began. No one reached out to them.

- And, most important, *no one invited them back!*

Does any of this sound familiar?

THE BIG QUESTIONS

Why do you think Catholics have historically been so lukewarm to actively seeking new members? Discuss this question with your ministry leadership team. Then, make it more immediate. Is outreach a ministry in which your parish should become actively engaged? If so, where and how will you begin? Since you will probably rule out an active raid on neighboring churches, how can you begin to identify visitors to your parish? Do you think that such visitors are there because they are looking for a parish? What can you do to make your parish the kind of place to which they will want to return? What can you do beyond reaching the occasional visitor?

BIBLIOGRAPHY AND ASSOCIATED RESOURCES

Researching materials for this chapter was somewhat difficult because of the very ambiguity of the meaning of Catholic outreach described earlier. Different resources exist for each area. "Catholics Reaching Out," for instance, was written specifically for inactive Catholics (addressed in this book in Chapter 14, "Inreach").

"Disciples in Mission," developed by the Paulist National Catholic Evangelization Association (PNCEA), "is a pastoral process that integrates the Sunday liturgies, small faith-sharing groups, catechesis, family activities, teen groups, planning, and follow-up activities into a coordinated parish-wide experience of evangelization. It fosters spiritual renewal by placing the missionary dimension at the heart of the community of faith-thus transforming it by the power of the gospel" (Quote taken directly from the program description on their Web site: www. disciplesinmission.org).

"Catholics Reaching Out" is also offered by the PNCEA. It is an extensive program aimed particularly at inviting inactive Catholics to return to the Church. Their Web site is www.pncea.org/programs/reachingout.aspx.

The main publishing body, Paulist Press, offers several helpful books:

From Maintenance to Mission: Evangelization and the Revitalization of the Parish by Robert S. Rivers, CSP (2005). The author offers practical ways to develop plans for evangelization in your parish.

Creating the Evangelizing Parish by Frank P. DeSiano, CSP, co-written with Kenneth Boyack, CSP, shows people in parish ministry what Catholic evangelization is all about. The Evangelizing Catholic also offers practical tools for reaching out.

Contact Paulist Press at:

Paulist Press
997 Macarthur Blvd
Mahwah, NJ 07430-9990
www.paulistpress.com

Plentiful resources also exist within the Protestant publishing realm on these issues. Begin with www.churchsolutionsmag.com. They offer many downloadable books and articles at very affordable prices. Begin with a search on two of their free articles: "Fifteen Reasons Why First-Time Guests May Not Return" and "Five Ways to Make Guests Feel Welcome." Another article, "Reaching Out to Men Creates Challenge," can be thought-provoking, whether you agree with all the author's premises or not.

CHAPTER 17

Task ← → Maintenance

Now as they went on their way, he entered a certain village, where a woman named Martha welcomed him into her home. She had a sister named Mary, who sat at the Lord's feet and listened to what he was saying. But Martha was distracted by her many tasks; so she came to him and asked, "Lord, do you not care that my sister has left me to do all the work by myself? Tell her then to help me." But the Lord answered her, "Martha, Martha, you are worried and distracted by many things; there is need of only one thing. Mary has chosen the better part, which will not be taken away from her."

Luke 10:38–42

Two duties lie at the core of every group. One function is problem-solving, to get its work done or achieve its goal (*task*). Certain members have skills that help to get this function done. The other is to take care of its members, to develop a sense of community, and improve the emotional life of the group (*maintenance*). Here, too, certain skills that members of the group possess help this function get done. Always monitor the task ← → maintenance balance. Neither task nor maintenance can be ignored. Neither can be seen as more important than the other. *Both roles are needed in every group.*

A favorite example is the group that plans to hold a spaghetti dinner. A group high on task and low on maintenance might hold the dinner, but its members will feel like they had been run over by a Nazi bulldozer! They might not continue as a group after the task is completed because members will not find it pleasant or enjoyable to belong to such a group. Conversely, a group high on maintenance and low on task will have difficulty accomplishing its objectives. Some members will become frustrated by the lack of progress. They will probably never get around to the spaghetti dinner, but most members will have had a great time just being with one another!

Good groups don't just happen. They don't work well by accident. The leader needs to have an awareness of how groups work and how to monitor this task/maintenance balance. While it would be great if every council or commission had a group dynamics expert present to teach and then keep an eye on this balance, most don't. The good news is that you don't need a rocket scientist to figure this out. The group leader simply needs to understand that different members can play different roles, what those roles are, and how to employ different techniques during group time together to assure that the task-maintenance balance is met.

If a group is to meet regularly, especially a group with a large agenda, it would serve their interests to help them become aware of this particular group dynamic. The brief exercise described below will help sensitize everyone to this issue.

◼ Task and Maintenance—How Can We Help Our Group Work Well Together?

Goals

1. To help all participants understand the two functions of all groups: task and maintenance.

2. To help everyone understand their own tendencies and how they can use them to make their group work better.

Time Required

30-45 minutes

Materials Needed

Two handouts, "Group Members With Task Roles" and "Group Members With Maintenance Roles."

A chalkboard and chalk, or easel, newsprint and markers.

Advance Preparation

The leader needs to have given thought to this group issue. Knowing that the group will be asked to brainstorm typical group activities, the leader must be able to identify quickly which ideas from the following group discussion belong in the task column and which belong in the maintenance column. (Do a Google search for "group task maintenance" for more help.)

What To Do

1. Introduce the activity. Explain that the goal of this session is to prepare the members of the group to work well with one another by exploring some skills that effective groups have. Encourage them to trust that this investment of time will have good payoffs as the group begins to delve deeply into its job. Thank them for their willingness to work together as effectively as possible. (Do not distribute the two handouts yet.)

2. Ask participants to brainstorm this question: "What have you seen people do in groups that you have belonged to that make some of them work better than others?" You might need to prime the pump a bit with a suggestion or two. Ask each person to take a moment to jot down answers to this question. Have your board or easel ready. Prepare to put their ideas into two columns, but don't put titles on the columns. So as to get contributions from all, ask each person to give one answer at a time, moving around the circle. As they give their answers, simply put them into appropriate columns: one for task and the other for maintenance. Remember: This is not about tricking anyone. And it's OK if one list is shorter than the other.

3. After members have given all their answers, title each column: "Task Roles" and "Maintenance Roles." Then, using your own stories and examples that came from the group, introduce the two functions that each group has. Invite conversation around this concept.

4. Distribute the two handouts and invite a comparison of the chalkboard lists and the printed lists. Give a few more moments of study. Then, explain that each member has different, unique gifts that can be called upon to monitor particular behaviors or use certain strengths and skills from each list to intervene when the group is struggling because of a particular imbalance. Again, invite sharing and reaction.

5. Ask members to identify their own best qualities, often ones from each list. It's OK if a person is heavy on just one list. Poll the group for the tendencies that appear most often on all lists. These, of course, will be the group's greatest strengths. Caution the group that these strengths can also be weaknesses unless they make certain that roles without any votes are covered as well.

6. Ask members to pair off to discuss which particular gift from each list they bring to the group and how those gifts can be used to strengthen its effectiveness.

7. Conclude the activity by inviting a larger group sharing. Ask the group to agree that it is OK (in fact, desirable) for any one person to intervene in the life of the group at particular moments in its future meetings to include a particular technique or to remind them that it is being ignored or missed. The good functioning of a group thus becomes the responsibility of every member, not just the leader.

8. Thank the group for their investment of time. Remind them again of the potential assistance this exercise will bring to their effectiveness.

9. As the group's leader, make a mental note to take them back to this activity during future meetings to reinforce the decision for each member to monitor particular group behaviors that help or hinder its functioning. Now, you can move on to other areas of group business.

GROUP MEMBERS WITH TASK ROLES

Members who perform task roles help get the business of the group done. These are the focused members, the "no-nonsense" people. They best understand the rational or "thinking and doing" part of the group's life.

FUNCTION (OR ROLE) WITHIN THE GROUP	PURPOSE OF THIS ROLE	TECHNIQUES OR SKILLS
Initiate	*Initially the leader, they start the discussion, give purpose or focus.*	*They suggest goals or solutions for getting the job done.*
Seek information or ask questions	*They help everyone understand the need for information. They can look at the big picture and challenge the group's suppositions.*	*They ask questions and seek clarifications.*
Give information	*They provide information relevant to the group's work.*	*They find or give facts related to the issue needed by the group. They avoid opinions.*
Clarify	*They help eliminate mix-ups around an issue.*	*They interpret comments. They help sort out issues or alternatives. They persuade others to be specific.*
Elaborate	*They think things through and show consequences. They try to reduce confusion.*	*They give examples. They build on suggestions. They explain the meaning of comments.*

GROUP MEMBERS WITH TASK ROLES

Members who perform task roles help get the business of the group done. These are the focused members, the "no-nonsense" people. They best understand the rational or "thinking and doing" part of the group's life.

FUNCTION (OR ROLE) WITHIN THE GROUP	PURPOSE OF THIS ROLE	TECHNIQUES OR SKILLS
Be critical	*They bring insights from similar events. They might be hard on issues but never on people.*	*They test assumptions and critically examine propositions. They take a contrarian position.*
Coordinate	*They offer adjustments to the issue when conflict occurs.*	*They look for alternatives to smooth the way an issue can be handled.*
Develop procedures	*They keep the group on track and make sure it follows the agenda.*	*They suggest where the group should go next. They remind the group when it gets off track.*
Summarize	*They bring ideas together and show how they are or are not connected.*	*They look for commonalities or contradictions in ideas. They watch what is being accomplished.*

continued on page 212

continued from page 211

GROUP MEMBERS WITH MAINTENANCE ROLES

Members who perform maintenance roles help make the members feel good about belonging. They look after the needs of the members. They tend to the communication channels. They best understand the emotional part of the group's life.

FUNCTION (OR ROLE) WITHIN THE GROUP	PURPOSE OF THIS ROLE	TECHNIQUES OR SKILLS
Encourage and affirm	*They try to get ideas from all. They give recognition.*	*They are warm and open to all. "That's a really good point." "We hadn't thought of that."*
Share feelings	*They encourage reactions to suggestions.*	*They help to keep it personal. "That happened to me once." They encourage others to share feelings.*
Relieve tension	*They can sense difficult moments and defuse conflict.*	*They help the group let off steam. They lighten the moment.*
Harmonize and compromise	*They help keep group togetherness and reconcile differences.*	*They offer compromises. They help conflicted members to "work it out."*
Facilitate	*They keep good communication, watch for contributions from all.*	*They look for ways to improve dialogue. They encourage contributions from silent group members.*
Set standards		

GROUP MEMBERS WITH MAINTENANCE ROLES

Members who perform maintenance roles help make the members feel good about belonging. They look after the needs of the members. They tend to the communication channels. They best understand the emotional part of the group's life.

FUNCTION (OR ROLE) WITHIN THE GROUP	PURPOSE OF THIS ROLE	TECHNIQUES OR SKILLS
Interpret	*They help members understand one another.*	*They paraphrase. They explain. "What I hear you saying is ..."*
Listen	*They are interested in the ideas of all members.*	*They place a high value on all members. They are open to everyone.*
Monitor for agreement	*They constantly watch for how close everyone is to agreement on the issue.*	*They watch for progress. They share where they see areas of agreement. They ask for a vote.*
Observer of the process	*They watch for moments of poor group interaction and intervene then.*	*They suggest ways to help the group get un-stuck or regain a sense of progress.*

THE BIG QUESTIONS

Is your group willing to examine its own effectiveness objectively by looking at its task-maintenance balance?

If your group has any ongoing dysfunctionality, such as an extremely obstructive member, can you locate a resource person who can come in to help resolve the problem?

Has this brief introduction to group dynamics suggested other areas where your group might need help? Who can assist you?

BIBLIOGRAPHY AND ASSOCIATED RESOURCES

Task-Maintenance balance can be found in nearly any comprehensive volume on group dynamics. One interesting place to begin is www.trainingforchange.org.

A Google search on "task maintenance roles" produces over five million hits.

CHAPTER 18

A Work-Pray-Play Balance in Parish Life

How Jesus Lived with Others

They devoted themselves to the apostles' teaching and fellowship, to the breaking of bread and the prayers. All who believed were together and had all things in common; they would sell their possessions and goods and distribute the proceeds to all, as any had need. Day by day, as they spent much time together in the temple, they broke bread at home and ate their food with glad and generous hearts. Now the whole group of those who believed were of one heart and soul, and no one claimed private ownership of any possessions, but everything they owned was held in common.

Acts 2:42, 44, 46; 4:32

The surveys taken across the U. S. having to do with church affiliation all point to the same thing. **Congregations that provide opportunities for authentic meaningful human relationships grow. Those that remain institutional and disconnected don't.**

Is it any surprise then that programs like Marriage Encounter and the Cursillo are successful? They flourish because they offer what the large church doesn't do very well. These "little churches" give opportunities in groups of a size that encourages true human relationships where members can share personal experiences about dealing with life, faith, and moral decision-making, how to deal with the whole range of daily decisions in light of the Word of God, and how to have a relationship with Jesus. Here members get to know others who live the same kind of life and who share the same struggles that they do. Members have a new kind of prayer experience, and unlike the rote recitation they all know so well, it is one that is authentic and comes from the heart. Adolescent retreat models like Teens Encounter Christ and the Search for Christian Maturity have understood this for years.

Those moments don't usually occur at Sunday Masses with the entire assembly, and, if that is the only encounter one has with the parish all week, then it should be no wonder that so many members drift away. Their church experiences become irrelevant and disconnected from their daily lives, leaving them with a feeling that there is little reason to stay. After all, probably no one will even notice when they leave. Parishes need to adapt and offer two different moments of church: one where small clusters do what isn't possible in large groups, and another where everyone comes together to celebrate their encounters with God and one another. Thus, the task is twofold. Here, we will deal with the formation and maintenance of small groups. (Improving the large parish eucharistic liturgical experience was already covered in Chapter 1.)

SMALL CHRISTIAN COMMUNITIES *

■ Learning from Small Christian Communities

In the early part of the twentieth century, small prayer groups as a subset of the parish began to appear throughout the church, not just in the United States. Over time, they took on the name "Small Christian Communities" (SCCs). This movement has continued to grow steadily. Many dioceses and countless parishes have embraced SCCs and offer organizational support to them.

Small Christian Communities have essentially been about prayer together. Their value to parish life cannot be overstated. They provide the vehicle for the most basic task of every Christian—communication with God. Many Web sites provide both a recommended standard format for these gatherings and weekly and seasonal details including specific Scripture passages as focus points. Of course, no one ever said that a particular SCC couldn't decide to socialize together as well. Many do. Nonetheless, the primary purpose is shared prayer. This chapter will not deal extensively with the prayer function, because so much is already written and can be found elsewhere.

NB! = IN CITY-BLOCK GATHERINGS

■ Moving Beyond SCCs

Take the little parish to the next step. Why not intentionally divide the parish into neighborhood sections—mini-parishes, if you will—with the intention of encouraging them not just to pray together but to play and work together as well. Ask your pastoral council members to help with this. They live across the parish and probably know its neighborhoods best. Depending upon the Catholic population density, each of these sections could be from a few blocks to a section of town. Keep them small enough, though, that the point isn't lost in the numbers. The goal is to provide opportunities for genuine people contact, a way for parishioners to meet others who live close to them and to share their Catholic experience with them. Invite two or three to act as Neighborhood Facilitators. You might look to a Marriage Encounter couple to help begin this. Their duties could include:

- Be faithful to the original purpose of SCCs: to provide prayer opportunities in small groups. *(INVITE TO RETREATS & BIBLE STUDY)*

- Organize occasional social gatherings, get-togethers, and other family-oriented events.

- Assist in identifying those who seem ready to serve as ministers within the parish.

- Bring news of parish events to everyone in the neighborhood. Help with sign-ups when necessary.

- Act as a liaison to bring news of parishioners to the parish staff (prayer needs, illness, moves into or out of the parish, or deaths).

OBS / SOCIAL NETWORKS / WEBS / EBELL

Bring these Neighborhood Facilitators together regularly for their own ministerial support and opportunity to share their experiences. Don't ask them to invent their job, provide them with the tools to do it. Many parishioners might be willing to help but might also not feel competent, especially for a new role not previously seen in parish life. Model for them the very experience you ask them to provide for others.

An alternate way of organizing SCCs would be around issues of commonality, like unmarried young adults, divorced Catholics, live-at-home college students, or empty-nesters. *HS STUDENTS*

The mantra must be: Little churches, yes; but always come back to the big church.

■ A Balancing Act

The underlying issue here is that of a balance in parish life—a balance of work-prayer-play. It is akin to the task-maintenance balance described in the last chapter but is approached somewhat differently. The task-maintenance balance is one of balance of *skills* among its members and committing to call upon those skills when needed. The work-pray-play balance is more one of determining the appropriate mix of *activities* in which the group engages. This balance needs to be constantly monitored, but in this case that monitoring is more likely done when the group is scheduling its meetings and activities; in other words, when the group is determining its life together. And, like the task-maintenance balance, this one, too, is needed in every group or organization, not just the church. If "task-maintenance" was Group Dynamics 101, "work-pray-play" is Group Dynamics 102.

The basic premise is this. **The foundation of faith development described in this book is built upon relational ministry. It is at the heart of evangelization, catechesis, and service. Ministerial leaders are called upon to model the lifestyle asked of all Christians, and, accordingly, ministerial leaders must do so in their own teams and groups as well. Everyone walking the walk of faith must be able to look at those leading the ministries of the parish and see an authentic practice of everything being preached. Relational ministry is at the heart of all this.**

Consequently, always keep a work-pray-play balance in every part of parish life. Begin by modeling this balance with all leadership groups, paid and unpaid. As each group develops its schedule of meetings and events for the year, make certain that it includes activities of all three types:

- *Work*—The most obvious purpose of most groups: getting the job done. Consider all organizational options for group effectiveness. If your group is large and has a large agenda, consider task forces or sub-committees so that the "grunt work" is done away from the main meetings, resulting in more time together for other purposes. Consider rotating meeting leadership among all members. This takes nothing away from the authority or mandate of the elected leader. Ask everyone to submit agenda items ahead of time, along with the amount of time needed for discussion and action. Ask the particular group leader to prepare a written agenda for everyone. In the case of complex agenda topics, prepare and distribute documentation in advance for better group effectiveness. Perhaps rotate the secretarial function as well.

- *Pray*—The part of group life together that will require the most assistance and monitoring. How many times has your group slipped past shared prayer because of the pressing agenda? Commit to an open-ended shared prayer at the beginning of each meeting. Invite prayer leadership on a rotating basis. Encourage creativity. Each member brings a different sensitivity to prayer to the group and should be encouraged to share that diversity. We can all learn from one another. And, the Lord speaks differently to each of us.

- *Play*—Another aspect of group life that the task-oriented among us will struggle with. Build occasional meetings around a barbecue or meal together. Celebrate important group milestones with a restaurant meal together. All the while remain sensitive to the family life obligations of each member of the group. Invite spouses and children to a Saturday afternoon of bowling, or an outing at a softball field at the neighborhood park. Remember that real life includes laughing—and crying—together. Always allow your groups the time to be completely authentic with one another, including time for the highs and the lows we all have.

However this balance is accomplished, it will only work to make your group healthier, more effective, and more balanced. Looking back to the previous chapter, your group will never burn out from task overload, but you will still get your work done. In the long term, your members will look back at their time together with joy and satisfaction. And, the prayer experiences together will enrich their personal Christian lives in ways that they will carry with them far beyond their service to your committee or group.

■ Let's Go Fishing!

Many years ago, I discovered FISH! I don't know whether to call it a company or a philosophy or a movement. It is, however, a company that offers consulting services to profit-making and non-profit organizations. It is built around a carefully crafted, yet fun-filled set of values that work in either world.

FISH! offers to *inspire* people to take action toward fully engaged living, *ignite* their creative spirit and *encourage* them to live into their full potential. (BBVOY)

They help their workshop participants to hold to four values:

- *Be There*, living in the present, really listening to others, always questioning "Who am I being while I'm doing what I'm doing?" and being respectful in all our interactions.

- *Play* by remaining childlike, keeping our curiosity alive and trusting it to lead to better solutions, and by doing so, believing that new ideas will arise.

- *Make Their Day* by being passionate about serving and mindful of the needs of others.

- *Choose Your Attitude* by living fully engaged lives, taking personal responsibility for our choices, utilizing all our talents, and remaining open to new learnings.

As an author and teacher, I have always been partial to people-oriented approaches that come out of the commercial sector. After all, within the church, one would expect such things. If such a way of doing business is embraced by the corporate world, it must work and be cost-effective. When one is found that both worlds endorse, like FISH! or Servant Leadership (see Chapter 4), it must be really good!

THE BIG QUESTION

At the beginning of this book is the phrase "It's hard to be a Christian by yourself!" The truth of that is at the heart of Jesus' message. Everything he taught us had to do with how we live our lives with one another and with God. What then must your parish do first to put a communal prayer life at the heart of every parishioner's experience? What can you do to provide organizational help and preparation to form smaller opportunities for Christian life together on a whole-person basis? What role should the pastoral council play in the leadership of this effort?

BIBLIOGRAPHY AND ASSOCIATED RESOURCES

Several Web sites have been developed that provide resources for SCCs. See www.buenavista.org to start. Google "small Christian communities" for a much more expansive list, literally thousands of resources. Ask your diocesan pastoral ministry office for additional support.

Check out www.charthouse.com if you find "FISH!" interesting.

CHAPTER 19

Who's Missing in Action?

Now the word of the Lord came to me saying, "Before I formed you in the womb I knew you, and before you were born I consecrated you; I appointed you a prophet to the nations." Then I said, "Ah, Lord God! Truly I do not know how to speak, for I am only a boy." But the Lord said to me, "Do not say, 'I am only a boy'; for you shall go to all to whom I send you, and you shall speak whatever I command you, Do not be afraid of them, for I am with you to deliver you, says the Lord." Then the Lord put out his hand and touched my mouth; and the Lord said to me, "Now I have put my words in your mouth."

Jeremiah 1:4–9

Many parishes are geared to the broad range in the middle of the bell curve, those married with children and the empty-nesters who frequently constitute the heart of ministry leadership. These are the easiest to reach and, in many places, the ones most desirous of parish involvement.

Try this exercise next Sunday. Get a clipboard and yellow pad. Go up to the choir loft and observe the congregation at several Masses.

Your first reaction may be the overall graying of the population. Try counting the various groups present: families with small or grade-school-aged children, teenagers, young adults, empty-nesters and other older parishioners. Are any wheelchair-confined persons in attendance? Or there any needing walkers?

What about members of the parish's minority groups, if that is apparent? Many observers of church life have suggested that Sunday morning is the most segregated hour in all of American life. Is that true in your parish?

Strain your neck from your high perch and try to identify all those who came in late and are leaning against the back wall. (Never mind the small children running down the aisle who have escaped the clutches of their parents. Or the occasional teen who rushes in to get a bulletin and learn who the priest is to prove to his parents that he was at Mass!)

Recruit other members of the leadership team and conduct this survey for several weeks at different Masses to get a representative view of who comes to Mass each week. What can you learn?

Did the count of small children even come close to the total in the parish school and the Saturday religion classes? Children won't be at Mass if their parents aren't. Where are all the parish teenagers? Could you count any significant number of unattached young adults—given even that many might attend college in distant places? Think of the older infirmed members of the parish whom you know personally—the ones who need wheelchair or walker assistance. How many of them did you see at Mass?

What conclusions can you reach from your observations? The picture is probably rather grim. The missing in action probably includes the entire spectrum—everyone from young families with small children, to teenagers, to young adults, to empty-nesters, able-bodied seniors, and the infirm. People are living longer and healthier than ever before. Just think about how your parents lived out their senior years. How different was it from the way your grandparents lived out theirs? Remember, too, all the ethnic groups of your parish. Perhaps a "Volume 2" of this book might deal with the whole litany of those missing in action just listed above.

Here, the focus will be solely on the young. One generalization true in nearly every parish is that the youth and young adult population is underrepresented, if not missing completely. We must begin this discussion with an acknowledgment. **Grade schoolers are not children of parishioners; they are parishioners. Teens are not children of parishioners; they are parishioners.** But where are they on Sunday morning? And sadly, many young adults, also parishioners, have begun what one author called their "holy hiatus."

CYO !!! THAT's WHERE

■ Peer Ministry

One easy solution to this problem comes to mind immediately. "Easy? Yes!" Of all the groups in the church who are "missing in action," youth and young adults can be reached most readily and, yes, most easily with *peer ministry*. For anyone who has spent time in youth ministry, this is a no-brainer. The mystery has always been why pastors and parish leaders can't or won't see this. For decades, peer ministry has been at the heart of successful programs for these age groups. And, yet, the idea just doesn't seem to ring true with older adults. Is it a question of trust? Is it one of not having the time or staff to give to the selection and mentoring of peer ministers? Is it the fact that peer ministers talk about life experiences and not church doctrine? Is it that they can surprise you with something not quite exactly doctrinally correct or precise? Probably some of each.

Nonetheless, one youth can reach another youth in ways that older adults cannot. It's just that simple. It works. Trust me.

In the discussion on evangelization in Chapter 3, I shared a story about a seventh- and eighth-grade retreat. A young man in high school, only a few years older, spoke to them about se[...] and the choices that he (and they) had to make each [...]

lives. He spared nothing. He talked about HIV and drug abuse and peer pressure and virginity and temptations. He spoke of his faith and his own journey, which had many peaks and valleys. I watched the students. They were hanging on to his every word. Do you think that they would have listened to you or me talk about virginity? They listened to him! Peer ministry works. Peer ministry is effective, whether teen to teen, or forty-year-old to forty-year-old, or eighty-year-old to eighty-year-old; but it is especially effective with young people. Peer ministry can be at the heart of the faith development process for your youth.

If youth are the most invisible part of your church population, begin with the junior high students. Does your parish have a grade school? Reach out to the seventh- and eighth-graders. If not, look to the confirmation or middle school religious education program. Begin a program for them that moves away from the classroom. Staff it with high school students. Invite a twenty-something to become the adult moderator. If your school works on alumni development, make sure that it includes reaching the eighth-graders while they are still in school, *before* they graduate. That work can do double duty. It can help with their potential alumni involvement, but it can also become the foundation for a high school youth ministry program. Let the program emphasize social interaction and group sharing on Christ-centered real life, growing-up issues. If you trust the faith development model described in Chapter 3, you can have confidence that doctrinal transmission will follow in due time.

■ Younger Kids

Reach out to the families in the parish school. Those folks are very busy raising families and scrambling to pay tuition. Even though many will attend Sunday Mass, they often have no more time for parish life and content themselves with meeting the many requests from the school for their time. Older families who remember their

own years with school-aged children may complain t ~~WEEKLY FAMILY MASS~~
younger families are not as visible in parish life as they once were,
but these are different times. *— WITH SOCIAL AFTERWARDS.*

#1 Offer a weekly Family Mass that involves lots of parents and
children. One parish faithfully rotates the planning and leadership
responsibilities for these Masses among the different classrooms of
the school and among the Saturday religious education classrooms
as well. Yes, it takes a lot of time and work to plan, but children
won't be at Sunday Mass if their parents aren't. Family Masses bring
everyone together. Again, make certain that equal time is given to
the religious education families who come every Saturday morning
or Wednesday afternoon. Many parishes have no Catholic school, *IF THERE IS NO SCHOOL*
and this is the only way to reach this group.

#2 Speaking of Saturday morning, why not offer coffee and conversation in the parish hall for parents during the same time their kids
are in classes? Instead of seeing them drop off their kids, offer an
opportunity for them as well. What better time to do something on
parenting challenges and skills, or helping to bring prayer life into
home life, or dealing with the endless war between siblings? Keep it
informal. *Do not hold the gathering in a classroom*, with neat rows
of desks designed for smaller bodies. (Try to fit an adult, slightly
overweight bottom on a fourth-grade chair.) Make it inviting and
easy and relevant. And, above all, invite someone who is already a
parent to lead these discussions. *ST A. DOES THIS*

#3 Another option for younger ones is *Liturgy of the Word for
Children*. In this program, children, perhaps those in grades 1-3,
leave the Sunday morning assembly after the introductory rite of
the Mass and go to a separate room for a more age-suitable proclamation and reflection of the Word, the Creed and the General
Intercessions. They then return to the Assembly for the remainder
of the eucharistic celebration. Several dioceses define the appropriate age level as those for whom the Lectionary for Masses with
Children is intended.

MORE LIKE 18-25

■ Those Out of High School

One study suggested that seventy percent of those between the ages of 23 and 30 drop out of their church for a time, and many spend more than a year away. That shouldn't come as a surprise. After all, they are going through a major time of life definition. They might be away at college or otherwise moving around, engaged with the task of defining careers. They probably graduated from college with staggering debt and are consumed with working enough hours each week to meet their loan payments. Many will hold ideological views at odds with older, more traditional organizations, like churches—or at least they perceive these places to be so. They may find the Sunday Mass tedious, boring, or irrelevant. They look around and see a very gray population and do not see others their age. They might simply be enjoying the freedom of no longer being under the scrutiny of their parents. Of course, this is not a new problem. For decades, some of them have returned when they marry or have children, but right now they are nowhere to be seen.

If you have any questions about where to find this age group, visit a gym or health club or a Starbucks on a Sunday morning. There you will find many young adults, perhaps some of your own.

One thing is certain. Parishes with flourishing high school programs, programs that integrate the teens into the broader life of the parish as well as providing them with their own unique activities, are far more likely to retain that connection as they become young adults—as long as the parish continues to reach them with equally relevant programs and opportunities for involvement.

The Sunday evening Mass is a natural for youth and/or young adults—with fellowship afterward. It makes sense on nearly every level. Many parishes discover that it is simply the right time for these groups. Coincidentally, the kind of Mass that makes sense to young adults also seems to work for others in the parish who choose that time for their weekly worship. Yes, it takes a lot of time and work to plan.

BAND?

One priest from San Francisco (now a bishop) offered a monthly "Ministry on Tap" gathering for young adults at a friendly neighborhood pub. It became an opportunity to gather, socialize, share concerns about living life in the modern world, and occasionally make a date. Or, if faith sharing in a bar is repugnant, Starbucks works just as well.

Programs often center on social gatherings like those just described and Christ-centered group sharing on very relevant life topics. Young adults are less likely to be imprisoned by the tyranny of peer pressure that accompanies earlier adolescence and can be much more open to shared prayer and other opportunities to experiment outside their "comfort zones." Many members of this generation are passionate about social justice issues and look for opportunities to make a real difference. The rise in popularity of volunteer vacations is the best indicator of this. Many young adults don't necessarily have the dollars to make contributions, but they look for opportunities to give of themselves with their time and work.

As much as peer ministry is a key to success with teens, self-direction is just as important with young adults. They are quite confident in their ability to set their own direction, and parish involvement needs to be much more subtle, of a moderator type rather than a director.

■ Social Networking on the Internet

Any discussion of youth or young adult ministry must deal with social networking Web sites, like www.myspace.com, www.facebook.com, and www.twitter.com. While this topic was mentioned in Chapter 12 on Alumni Development, social networking has become so pervasive that it requires much more attention. Social networking sites, like the three mentioned above, provide members the opportunity to communicate informally with their friends.

It's a spontaneous stream of consciousness, and it's instantaneous. No need to pick up a telephone—just type in a few words on your BlackBerry or iPod and it's out there in cyberspace. "Blogging" is like that, too. The only difference is that many other Web sites—like your church's Web site, perhaps—offer blogging without going to one of the three mentioned. FYI: "Blog" is a short form of "web log." With blogging, the user can follow a stream of conversation (sometimes called a "thread") and add comments to it.

Social networking is not unique to the young, but it is ubiquitous in this age group. They have grown up in a technology-dominated world and most absolutely live for the instantaneous contact of social networking computer activities.

If you question this approach, remember that Pope Benedict XVI and the Vatican recently established a Youtube channel! (Go to www.youtube.com, type "Pope Benedict" in the search box, and be amazed.) Blogging, too, is as natural as picking up the telephone. Your parish Web site will either attract young people or turn them off completely, depending upon how well it is constructed. And don't waste postage on snail mailings to them. E-mail, e-mail, e-mail—that's the way to reach youth and young adults.

Becoming involved in social networking admittedly takes some getting used to. Let me share my own experience with it.

A Personal Story

In my own parish, I have responsibility for alumni development at the school. We know that Epiphany School has graduated over 5,000 children during its seventy-plus years, but we have lost contact with most of them. *At the recommendation of an eighth-grader,* I joined Facebook to find them. The eighth-grader, named Ricky, told me that he was aware of hundreds of Epiphany people on that site. He explained to me that Facebook members declare their interests and join sub-groups within the larger community. Ricky said that Facebook already contained interest groups of different Epiphany classes and that they used it to stay connected with one another. One general group called "Epiphany Eagles" has nearly 350 members!

I immediately realized the wisdom of Ricky's suggestion. Facebook would be an invaluable tool to reach graduates and reconnect with them. There are some downsides to these sites as well, however. A brief explanation is necessary. Most Facebook users have restrictions on their personal page, limiting access to it to those whom they have approved. Thus, when I discover an alumnus on Facebook, it is necessary for me to ask to become their "Facebook friend." I do so by introducing myself to them in a message and explaining my purpose. In nearly every case, I am accepted into their circle, at which time I become an invisible observer of their comments—about life, about school today, about family life, about their friends, about *everything*! These comments can be seen only by those within their personal circle of Facebook friends. For some of them, their use of coarse language to express frustrations about doing homework at 2:45 AM, or unhappiness with the progress of a romance, is sometimes jarring.

Taking on this kind of ministry is time-consuming to be sure. Be warned that the number of your e-mails will increase geometrically as you go deeper and deeper into these groups. The payoff, however, will be opportunities to engage young people in a place and in a way that makes sense to them. If you doubt this, just look around at malls, at coffee shops, everywhere, for the number of young people typing in text messages.

THE BIG QUESTIONS

Because of the unique differences found in youth (both middle school and high school) and young adults, perhaps the most important questions here have to do with selecting the right ministers from your parish population. A particular skill set is not nearly as important as an openness to the age group, a transparent respect for them, and an authenticity and honesty in relating to them. Being in a particular age range is not important. Some of the most effective youth ministers I have ever met have been older adults. Who, then, are the potential youth and young adult ministers in your parish?

BIBLIOGRAPHY AND ASSOCIATED RESOURCES

Liturgy of the Word for children is an ecclesiastically approved liturgical model. A Google search on "Liturgy of the Word for children" produced 1,750,000 hits. Consequently, you will have no problem finding lots of Internet resources on the topic. First, however, contact your diocesan liturgy office for guidance.

Web addresses for the social networking sites discussed are shown within the text. By the time you read this, others may have appeared. The Internet is a very dynamic resource. Do you want to know which site is hot right now? Just ask your sixteen-year-old.

CHAPTER 20

Consensus-Seeking
and Other Complicated Ways to Reach Agreement

> Then the apostles and the elders, with the consent of the whole church, decided to choose men from among their members and to send them to Antioch with Paul and Barnabas. They sent Judas called Barsabbas, and Silas, leaders among the brothers.
>
> Acts 15:22

Just mention the word "consensus" in any group of leaders; someone will swear *by* it and someone else will swear *at* it! Query each of the two, and their success and horror stories will provide a ready-made list of the pros and cons of this method of decision-making.

Consensus as a decision-making tool is not the product of some twentieth-century touchy-feely movement. It has been known for centuries! The Iroquois Federation, a council of Native American tribes in the area now known as New York State, was believed to employ consensus as early as the mid-1100s! The Mennonites used it in the 1500s, and the Quakers in the 1600s. In fact, the Mennonites even claim biblical roots for consensus, pointing out that the decision making of early Christians described in the Acts of the Apostles clearly show consensual patterns.

A Google search in the word "consensus" will produce many different definitions and descriptions, perhaps because its difficulty in execution makes it subject to modification. The methods proposed here, a relatively pure, unadulterated form, work well in ministerial groups where members are of good will and generally like mind. If you are interested in studying consensus more deeply, the Quaker model is closest to this model. At its best, consensus is a win-win method of reaching group decisions. No one loses.

WHEN GROUP HAS RESEARCHED A SOLUTION AND NONE IS KNOWN

■ Its Characteristics *(THERE IS A TIME AND A PLACE FOR CONSENSUS)*

All group members share a common vision.

Each member has a willingness to trust in the good will of all members.

Each member shares responsibility for the decision-making process.

Each person shares responsibility for maintenance of the group.

Group members need to separate issues from personalities. Holding a grudge or being annoyed or angry with another member must be resolved outside the discussion of an issue.

The proposer of an idea must be open to compromise, trusting that the group can formulate a better proposal than any one person can.

The leader does not serve as the person in charge but as the facilitator of the discussion. Of course, if the group is truly democratic, the leader (typically but not necessarily the pastor) may relinquish the facilitator role and allow it to rotate among all the staff. Since a facilitator, by definition, has no implicit power, such a shift would simply allow group facilitation to move among all members and provide variety in styles.

The duties of the facilitator include:

- Helping the discussion to take place,

- Making certain that every member understands the issues,

- Monitoring the workings of the group so that every member listens to and understands the others and is able to take part, and

- Looking for the moment when the group is ready to seek closure to the issue.

If an allocation of time has been agreed to before the discussion begins, the facilitator needs to monitor the time and keep members aware of an impending closure. (In that instance, the group can agree to an extension of discussion time, as appropriate.) The facilitator is an equal member of the group but may, in the interest of neutrality, choose to defer from offering a personal opinion as long as it is expressed by another member.

The decision finally reached is owned by the entire group and not solely by the leader. No one feels out of the loop.

Consensus seeks unity, not unanimity.

■ The Pros

Members come to know each other and each other's values more clearly.

The process ensures that each person speaks to the issue.

Consensus does not violate the fundamental values of any member of the group.

It helps each member to see more sides of a question and/or other alternatives.

It recognizes the reality of synergy—that is, a group is capable of producing a creative sum greater than the collective efforts of the individual members. It calls upon the wisdom of the group. A well-functioning group will make a better decision than an individual will.

A real decision is made only when all members of the group—even those who might have originally disagreed with the proposal—persist in that decision to see it through to completion.

Consensus works best in small groups (like parish staffs or pastoral councils).

Consensus works best when it is the end result of group formation and training and where the group holds a shared vision of its purpose and values.

It acknowledges the presence of the Holy Spirit in the group. Hopefully, the Spirit will guide members so that a Spirit-filled group will make better decisions than a Spirit-less one.

It assures complete group agreement on a position or issue. ("Assures," not "guarantees." There are never any guarantees in a group process.)

■ The Cons

It takes longer to reach agreement than a vote does and may be unworkable for urgent matters.

The group may be unwilling to act when one or more members are away, such as vacation.

Dominant, extremely verbal members can control the group.

One strong objector, or a small group of objectors, can destroy the process in two specific ways:

- This power, even when used accidentally, gives a significant advantage to those resistant to change. It can lead to preservation of the status quo.

- Second, inflexible members can intentionally block a proposal and create disruption, causing the group to be held hostage to views held by one or a few.

Consensus-seeking may lead to "groupthink," where participants change their views to accommodate what they think the will of the group is. This can lead to situations where a decision is reached that no one actually supports, called pseudo-consensus.

Moments may arise in the life of the group where agreement cannot be reached. Diametrically opposing views may be held on both sides that are ultimately irreconcilable.

■ The Process

Clearly, members of the group need to have agreed upon operating norms before decision making begins. This might occur at an annual retreat held before the calendar year begins. These norms might include points like these.

- Members agree to let the Holy Spirit work within the group. Some will call it the Holy Spirit. Others will call it synergy. We are talking about the same reality: a well-functioning group can accomplish more than what its individual members can do alone.

- Members agree to avoid arguing in order to win as individuals. What is "right" is the best collective judgment of the group as a whole.

- Conflict on ideas or solutions should be viewed as helping rather than hindering the process of seeking consensus—but only if all members have a basic respect for each other and practice open, positive communication and feedback.

- The best results of group process flow from a mixture of logic, information, and emotion. Judgments about what is best include the feelings of members about the issue at hand and the decision-making process.

One member lays the proposal upon the table for discussion and decision and gives up sole ownership of the proposal so that the group may modify it to reach consensus. (Providing advance documentation for more complex proposals can also be helpful, allowing for more study and reflection.) The proposal is seen as clay that will possibly be molded and shifted as needed. Of course, the original proposer is not excluded from this process.

The facilitator elicits from the proposer enough information that everyone understands what is being offered. Brainstorming various options can be appropriate at this early stage.

The facilitator polls each person to offer initial concerns or expressions of agreement.

Silence does not mean assent. Personality styles differ. One individual, reflective by nature, might sit and watch the exchange, never offering a viewpoint until queried. The facilitator should frequently poll *all* members throughout the process so as to discover areas where resolution is needed rather than be surprised later when there is a supposition of agreement.

The facilitator is responsible for balancing the discussion so that extremely verbal members, or those more passionately committed or opposed to the proposal do not dominate the process. This usually means limiting the number of times one person can speak until everyone has spoken.

While the entire process is the responsibility of the whole group, the facilitator has a special duty to monitor that an objector is doing so out of true conviction and not out of selfishness or a personal agenda.

The proposal belongs to the group and is no longer in the hands of any one person. The facilitator continues to seek new ideas and modifications, constantly articulating adjustments and fine tuning, all the while making certain that all members share the direction that change is taking, and at the same time attempting to move the group toward an acceptable solution. All points of view, including those of the former minority, are heard and built into the ever-changing proposal. As each modification is offered, it is important to check that the now modified idea still meets the needs of the original proposal.

The facilitator asks for all concerns to be raised until there is a clear sense of the group.

In a discussion around a complex issue, or one with more than one strong point of view, the facilitator will probably poll for consensus several times. This allows unresolved points to rise to the surface so that discussion stays focused on remaining differences.

If the group reaches an impasse where agreement seems impossible, the facilitator can call a short break to allow emotions to cool, or perhaps even postpone the continuation of the process until the next meeting for the same reason.

Since the expectation of the consensual model demands that the group has undergone significant team-building and goal-setting, the facilitator will probably employ communication strategies like active listening.

When the proposal, however modified, slightly or significantly or not at all, is satisfactory to everyone, a final polling is taken and consensus has been reached. The end result is a decision that belongs to all members of the group. When consensus works, there is no win-lose. Everyone wins, no one loses. Many believe that, however difficult to achieve, consensual decision-making is the **only** appropriate method for parish leaders to use.

THE BIG QUESTION

Consensus will work only when a group shares common values and when each member has established a positive trust level with all other members. This comes partially from the selection of members of a team—not necessarily members who all think alike but members who share a common vision—but that is seldom possible. It also comes from prayer and formation opportunities within the group. If you want to move to consensual decision making, what steps must you take to help prepare the group? What training and formation opportunities can you find to bring your group to a readiness for consensus? Can you find outside facilitators who can bring an impartial leadership to your group process? How will you know when the group is ready?

BIBLIOGRAPHY AND ASSOCIATED RESOURCES

A Google search on the word "consensus" produced 40,700,000 hits! Good luck! While countless references on consensus, both positive and negative, are cited, very few actual books on this subject could be found. Most search links were articles or definitions of the word. A more productive approach seems to be a search for the words "group dynamics" (only 15,800,000 hits!). Most print material on group dynamics will contain some information on consensus.

The Formal Consensus Web site (www.consensus.net), while offering print material for sale and workshops, provides helpful information as well.

CHAPTER 21

The Importance of Being Two-Faced

Learn where there is wisdom, where there is strength, where there is understanding, so that you may at the same time discern where there is length of days, and life, where there is light for the eyes, and peace.

Baruch 3:14

The Romans had a god named Janus. He was the god of the beginnings and endings (and of doors). He gave his name to our month called January. He had two faces: one looking forward and another looking back. Ministry leaders should be that way, too. Everyone should have two faces, one always looking forward to new and exciting things and another looking back, always evaluating all that has gone before

In the press of daily business, a careful and well-developed planning process can easily be overlooked or put aside. "After all," the leaders say, "we have too much going on, and everybody seems happy with things as they are. Why do we need to change anything?" The status quo can prevail by sheer default.

■ Some Definitions

This model is built around these assumptions:

1. The process lasts all year. It has no end point. It is circular. The formal annual process requires a constant looking forward (always identifying future needs) and a simultaneous looking backward (always evaluating existing programs). The weekly process of implementing regular programs always means fine-tuning them to meet current needs.

2. The process takes a shared commitment and ownership by everyone. Many elements of this model will be new to some participants. For others, such a complex structure will seem unwieldy and perhaps artificial. Take frequent "temperature checks" among your team to make certain that everyone is comfortable and on board. *Silence does not necessarily mean assent.*

3. **Decide very early how each component of parish leadership will participate in the planning process.** Since the staff is the principal "doing" part of the organization, all other components need to be involved at all stages: the pastoral council, finance council, education, liturgy, and all other committees. You need to identify all such bodies in your own parish and include them throughout the entire circular process. Perhaps not every member of every group will participate in every step of the process, but a collective decision needs to be made before adopting this process to guarantee full ownership of all decisions.

4. It sometimes seems too time-consuming. This model has no formal end point, where the group can close the book on planning until next year. For some, this will seem like a waste of time.

5. It requires mutual accountability. There is little place in this model of change for pure idea people. Few of us have large enough leadership teams to have such a luxury! At its heart is the role of the "lead agent." This is usually the person who puts forth a particular plan or idea. Once the group reaches an agreement on its future, then that same person may well be called upon to lead its implementation. Start by appointing a lead agent for the planning process itself, someone who believes completely in the value of planning, someone who will stay with the task and gently nudge each member all along the way toward mutual accountability.

6. Change usually happens very subtly. It's not often one dramatic event. Demographic changes occur that way. Ethnic mixes don't usually change overnight. Neither do age changes. Leaders need to keep a keen eye open to sense these kinds of changes. For instance, at the author's parish, when there were no longer any Irish who could cook the corned beef for the annual St. Patrick's Dinner and the event was being handled by the Filipino Society, it didn't take a rocket scientist to realize that change had happened. It had, in fact, occurred very slowly, almost imperceptibly, over a period of many years.

7. In most parishes, while the fiscal year begins in July and ends in June, the "program year" or "pastoral year" begins in September with the start of the new school year.

8. Be sensitive also to the liturgical year, which begins of course with the First Sunday of Advent. While some programs fit by nature within certain liturgical seasons (ie, Days of Recollections during Advent or Reconciliation Services during Lent), always monitor needs springing from special requests coming from your Diocese or the Vatican (i.e., a Holy Year).

9. This planning model peaks in March of each year. (Notice that I didn't say "finishes.") The soundness of this schedule will probably become apparent as the structure is studied. March was selected for the planning retreat so as to have adequate time do two things:

- Address fiscal concerns raised by new programs and make any necessary budgetary adjustments, and
- Before the summer begins, "flesh out" any programmatic changes that need to begin in September.

■ Steps in the Annual Planning Process

September and October Begin the new parish pastoral year

November The group begins to identify potential issues for the Annual Planning Retreat (APR); lead agents are assigned for all issues.

December Each lead agent researches the topic to determine feasibility; allow adequate time early in the month so that a normal break from leadership meetings can happen for Christmas

January Topic positions are presented, including a projection of the amount of time needed at the APR to resolve the question; the group prioritizes the topics; they agree and set a workable agenda for the APR

February Each lead agent continues to develop the topic and creates printed agenda material for advance distribution to all group members; agenda material is distributed to all for advance study; other duties for the APR, like prayer leadership, social activities, and meals, are assigned

March The Three-day Planning Retreat is conducted

April Each lead agent is then responsible for preparing a final written report on the topic based upon the group's action at the APR;

communication on budget impact of all agenda items is presented; otherwise, keep April (or late March) light to allow for Easter responsibilities

May Each lead agent seeks placement at a future group meeting by projecting a time that is both suitable for final presentation and relevant for potential implementation of the group's recommendations; set the annual September-August calendar

June Use June to wrap up all end-of-the-year issues and do advance work for activities occurring in early September

July and August R & R months; face the reality that many folks will be busy with family vacations; even if they aren't, it might not be a bad idea to lighten their parish responsibilities with a break before jumping back into "Full Speed Ahead" in September

September and October Begin the new parish pastoral year

November The group begins again to think about the annual planning cycle, beginning to identify potential issues for the Annual Planning Retreat ("APR"); lead agents are assigned for all issues; otherwise, keep planning activities light so that there is adequate time to continue all existing activities and changes.

And so, the circle continues.

■ Learning How Your Group Works

It should be very clear from this discussion and the previous one on group decision-making that group formation is a key element that must occur before either step can be taken. Don't rush into either task prematurely and set yourself up for failure. Many groups have discovered that an important issue is learning how each member of the group works best. We are all different persons, with our own strengths and weaknesses, our own quirks and idiosyncrasies. **Understanding and accepting each member is fundamental to group**

success. Accepting differences in members as strengths and not weaknesses will move a group from dysfunctionality to success.

Many methods have been developed to reach this point, but one has been used successfully for many years by thousands of church groups, especially staffs. The Myers-Briggs Type Indicator (MBTI) is a questionnaire completed by each member of the group. One reason for its popularity is that, while categorizing personalities into sixteen archetypes, it accepts each as "normal," making no claims than one is superior to another. Thus, no member of the group can fear that personal "quirks" will be viewed as pathological. The MBTI is built upon the typological theories developed by Carl Jung in the 1920s. Simply stated, while Freud showed the framework within which all human minds work, Jung showed us the different ways that people perceive the world and make decisions. By understanding ourselves and others, we can make our group become more effective in its work together.

The MBTI is built upon four pairs of preferences or dichotomies. A very brief description of these pairs follows:

- Am I an *extravert* or *introvert*? (Put aside the everyday connotations of these words, and don't worry about the unfamiliar spelling "extravert.") Do I draw my energy from action and involvement with others? Or do I prefer reflection and the interior world? (E or I)

- Am I *sensate*, relying only upon hard, tangible facts, or *intuitive*, trusting in intangible hunches and future possibilities? (S or N)

- Am I a *thinker*, tending to decide things from a more detached standpoint, or a *feeler*, tending to come to decisions by associating or empathizing with the situation? (T or F)

- Am I a *judging* type, preferring to "have matters settled," or a *perceiving* type, preferring to "keep decisions open?" (J or P)

In each of the four pairings, an individual with a very high point score will have a very dominant personality within the pairing. Someone with a lower score will be seen as having a more balanced personality, with a better ability to understand opposites.

In each case, both are good, neither is bad. These four pairings offer the sixteen archetypes mentioned above, made up of one letter from each pairing. An individual could be an INTJ, or an ESFP, or any other of the sixteen possible combinations. (At MBTI gatherings, participants wear their name tags, proudly announcing their own type—and perhaps looking to make a date with another similarly disposed!) Since they are all "normal," Katharine Cook Briggs and her daughter, Isabel Briggs Myers, held that groups would work more effectively if all members came to understand the preferred style of one another and could accept these differences as group strengths. If you think about the members of your staff in MBTI terms, you will readily understand how sharing around them could make the group more effective.

You will find trained facilitators of the MBTI in most larger communities. The instrument is too complex, with many layers of interesting and insightful ramifications, to be self-administered. Do your group a service by locating someone who can process the MBTI with your members. Check with the pastoral ministry resource person in your diocesan office for assistance.

If you have no experience with the MBTI, you may gain insights into the approach by reading David Kiersey's book, *Please Understand Me.* Kiersey offers a shorter, self-administered questionnaire called the Kiersey Temerament Sorter, which is built upon the same psychological theories, although not officially connected to the MBTI. This book might help you decide upon the value of the actual MBTI, administered and processed by a professional, for your leadership team.

THE BIG QUESTIONS

Just as with a decision to employ the consensual decision-making model, a major issue here will be an agreement of all members of the group to commit the time necessary over the long term to make this model work. Are all members willing to do so? The staff and pastoral council are central to this process, but who are the other leadership groups in your parish that need to be included? What will be their degree of involvement?

The decision to adopt such a comprehensive planning model will go hand-in-hand with a choosing your group's decision-making method: consensus or voting.

Making these two decisions simultaneously may seem like "biting off too much," but they do seem to belong together. The organization's leader may need to carefully decide if he or she is ready to invite such broad sharing into his or her leadership style.

BIBLIOGRAPHY AND ASSOCIATED RESOURCES

Google "goals and objectives" and "management by objectives." You will come upon many interesting and often helpful Web pages and sites. While almost all of them will be business-related, you will find lots of adaptable materials. One particularly interesting site is www.12manage. com and one particular page therein, www.12manage.com/methods_ smart_management_by_objectives.html.

Management by Objectives (MBO) was originally developed in the 1950s by Peter Drucker, a well-known author on organizational issues. His best-known book, *The Practice of Management*, is still in print and offered in paperback by online sellers like www.amazon.com.

The Myers-Briggs Type Indicator has been in use for decades. Its publisher, Consulting Psychologists Press, claims that it is used by over two million people each year. Check with your diocesan pastoral ministry office for local resources. Or, do a Google search for "MBTI [name of your city]." Go to the official Web site (www.myersbriggs.org) for additional information.

Keirsey, David, and Marilyn Bates, *Please Understand Me: Character and Temperament Types*. Del Mar, California: Prometheus Nemesis.

CHAPTER 22

What Are the Chief Marks of the Church?

> "It is the terror of the Church. I hate her, and still I can't leave her. I love her, and still I can't live with her in peace."
>
> Father Teleman, a character in *The Shoes of the Fisherman*

In the film *The Shoes of the Fisherman,* based on a book by Morris West, Oskar Werner played a young priest transparently patterned after Teilhard de Chardin. (In that movie, Anthony Quinn played the Soviet-born pope.) Werner's character had been called to Rome to defend his avant-garde writing. Tortured with frustration, he reacted in anguish. Haven't we all known that torment at one moment or another? What makes this church at times so easy to hate and so difficult to love? The tug of war between conscience and obedience remains an eternal question for many believers.

In 313 AD, the Roman Emperor Constantine removed all penalties for being Christian and effectively legalized Christianity in the ancient world. As he consolidated his power throughout both the eastern and western parts of the Roman Empire, he sought to "standardize" Christian practices and beliefs, especially since one particular heretical movement known as Arianism was gaining acceptance. He convened the first ecumenical council, the Council of Nicaea, a city in Asia Minor (now Turkey) in 325 AD. (He had not yet founded Constantinople.) The most memorable product of that council was the Nicene Creed, still in use today. Later, at the First Council of Constantinople in 381 AD, the sentence "We believe in one, holy, Catholic and apostolic Church." was added; and the concept of the Four Marks of the Church came into use.

Even before that time, the idea behind the Four Marks had been found in church writings. They were referenced by St. Ignatius, a very early church Father and only the third bishop of Antioch. Ignatius lived in the years just following Jesus' death. Tradition even maintains that as a child he had been held in Jesus' arms and blessed. Thus, for over nineteen hundred years, Christians and later Roman Catholic Christians, have professed a belief in these four characteristics of the church.

Baltimore Catechism Question #155: What are the chief marks of the Church? A.: The chief marks of the Church are four: It is One, Holy, Catholic (or universal), and Apostolic.

The question still echoes in my memory. From catechism class at Sacred Heart School, Granite City, Illinois, in the long ago, I know that the church is One, Holy, Catholic, and Apostolic. The Four Marks are indelibly etched into my mind. From many visits to Rome, I know, too, that the church is one, holy, catholic, and apostolic. But what does this mean in real life? Sister taught us that a "mark" is a sign. Thus, she said, the marks of the church are in fact the visible signs or characteristics of the church.

How do we remain faithful to this church of two thousand years' duration and still not scream in torment as Oskar Werner did? Where do we find these marks? Why are they important to the church? Why are they relevant to our discussion of the parish?

■ A Personal Story

Wednesday: Day One of the Pilgrimage

It was April 1984. John Paul II had convened the first of many Youth Jubilees. We marched in an incredible torchlight procession down Via della Conciliazione. From Castel Sant'Angelo, 100,000 of us, from around the world, having first encountered one another as strangers, we marched to Piazza San Pietro and became family, as we met one another, the church, and the pope.

Saturday: Day Four

Nearly five hundred thousand pilgrims swarmed into Piazza San Pietro in the waning sunlight to hear the pope, to see the pope, to be with the pope. The Jubilee was coming to an end. Tickets were useless. A tidal wave of humanity poured in between the colonnades into the piazza. More accurately, we were swept in. Surrounded by frenzied Italians and gigantic palm and olive branches, we stood in awe as the sun set over San Pietro. Pope John Paul II and Mother Teresa appeared and transfixed us with their words and their presence.

The Church is one.

Friday: Day Three

We watched a dramatic moonrise over the Colosseum, one hundred fifty thousand of us. We listened in silence. The words of Mother Teresa, John Paul, and Brother Roger of Taizé brought the Stations of the Cross to us face-to-face, with immense immediacy. They echoed against the stones bloodied by martyrs. They penetrated our bodies and hearts and souls.

Someday, later in our lives, we will look back and say that we prayed with Saint Teresa of Calcutta and Saint John Paul II.

The Church is holy.

Another pilgrim and I stood together on a rise in Piazza San Pietro near the colonnades, in a Woodstock-sized crowd commonplace in Rome. "Five hundred thousand faces—all different." I was stunned at the thought. It was absolutely true! Five hundred thousand different stories! Five hundred thousand circuitous routes that had all converged right here, right now. Songs in many languages; sharing the Sign of Peace with others from Thailand, France, Niger, Pakistan, and, of course, Italy. Always, everywhere, the Italians! Overhead was the Goodyear blimp!

The Church is catholic.

Saturday: Day Four

We celebrated the Eucharist in the Catacombs of Santa Priscilla. A spooky, zombie-like tiny nun with a portable amplifying system was our guide. She spoke in a flat, emotionless voice—hollow, cold, rehearsed, with no inflection—that moved through the tunnels. It was an echoless, still place, and the sound of our words and the shuffling of our feet were lost in the soft tufa walls at every bend and corner. The cool silence there and the timeless, haunting words of an ancient liturgy worked to make all of us keenly aware of our past and our heritage. That same timelessness of those words, though, especially as prayed by our friend and priest, Father Mike, also reminded us of our present. Each person there, looking around at others, was aware of the remarkable experience we were all having together in this incredible city.

Palm Sunday: The Final Day of the Pilgrimage

On that Palm Sunday, the largest crowd ever assembled in the City of Rome came to the steps of St. Peter's. Near the portable, outdoor altar, I scanned the panorama of this enormous mass of humanity. In what seemed like an incredibly long distance, the pope—a mere speck of red—stood at the foot of the obelisk in the center of the piazza. He chanted an ancient blessing over the palms. The words, the robes, the chant—they were all the same. The scene was the same. Except for the television cameras and the blimp over-

head, one could wonder if this was the twentieth cen[
sixteenth.

There is a room off the side of St. Peter's in which are listed the names of the scores and scores of popes buried in that church. (Not all popes are.) To observe that the names of John XXIII and Paul VI and the two John Pauls had been chiseled so recently brought about a jolting sense of mortality. Conversely, I observed that some others were cut into that marble a very long time ago. I was thrown back into history to the beginning of the church as I visualized the procession of popes across the centuries. There is still a great amount of space on that marble wall.

The Church is apostolic.

The church is one, holy, catholic, and apostolic. In Rome, the four marks are present and seen daily, as wave after wave of pilgrims come to experience their roots and their faith. "All right," you acknowledge. "This interesting travelogue of Rome arguably makes a case that the traditional marks of the church can be found in Rome. But why is this important to us today? Even more important, why is this relevant to a discussion of the characteristics of a great parish? After all, what happens is Rome sometimes seems to have little connection to life in our parish."

Traditionalist Catholics frequently hold the Four Marks up as if to say to Protestants "We're the one true church and you're not!" That is not the issue here, however. The more important matter in this discussion is that the four marks can serve as a checklist to evaluate the parish. In other words, if the four marks have been important for nearly two millennia in describing the universal church, then shouldn't they also be used to describe the local church? They are or ought to be at the heart of a great parish. The very manifestation of these characteristics will determine how great or excellent the parish is. Warning: this can be a daunting and very challenging activity.

How are we one, holy, catholic, and apostolic in our local parish?

THE BIG QUESTIONS

How are we one? How do we bring about unity and understanding among the many small communities in our parish? Do we maintain a unity of doctrine, in a way that does not seek to blend different approaches into one approach? Can we differentiate between unity and uniformity? Do all small communities within the parish share the same sacramental beliefs? How do we help all our small communities strengthen their commitment to our Holy Father?

How are we holy? Does our priest provide a model of a Christ-centered life that can animate all parishioners to deeper personal spirituality? Is our life as a parish immersed in prayer? Do we offer individual spiritual direction? What about opportunities to explore the writings of our Church Fathers and great saints? Do we have parish retreats and days of recollection? Is the parish open to all forms of spiritual expression? Are enduring structures present that facilitate personal spiritual growth?

How are we catholic (or universal)? How do we respect the uniqueness and diversity of the many small communities that make us whole? How do we avoid the desire to bring the others into *our* parish, instead of constantly inviting everyone to reinvent the parish so that it responds to all? How do we respect the cultural differences we find and honor the many different insights into spirituality?

How are we apostolic? How faithful are we to the two millennia of stories and tradition of our great church? Our bishop can trace his lineage of succession back to the apostles. Our pastor can trace his lineage back to the founding pastor of the parish. Have we ever looked at the vision that the founders of our parish had as an anchor point for our contemporary direction? How do we celebrate our heritage? How do we keep it known to our parishioners?

After all the philosophical and programmatic discussions of the these twenty-two chapters, in many respects, these four marks make a church great or mediocre.

BIBLIOGRAPHY AND ASSOCIATED RESOURCES

The online Catholic encyclopedia offered by www.newadvent.org offers lengthy theological treatises on the four marks of the church. They sprang from the work of the Council of Nicaea, held in 325 AD, but were not actually formulated until the First Council of Constantinople in 381 AD.

There were many different editions of the famous Baltimore Catechism, but they all contained the question and answer quoted earlier in this chapter.

How to Get There

You have endured almost 73,000 words trying to educate, stimulate, entertain, challenge, cajole, amuse, and otherwise nudge you into making your parish greater than it already is. Congratulations! Perhaps you could relate to my personal stories. Perhaps the Big Questions have given you an agenda for change. Whatever you do, don't stop now. Read on and get ready to move forward.

Oh yes: why twenty-two steps? Life does not come at us in neat orderly batches. We live in the church of the human condition. Life can be disorderly, discordant, even chaotic—and that is often the best of times! Each day brings a new batch of surprises. And they don't often come in predictable groups. Why twenty-two? There could have been fourteen, or twenty-seven or one hundred thirty-one. In the course of writing this book, the number has varied from seventeen to twenty-eight! You will begin to discover the number that works for your parish, but probably not yet.

I began diocesan work in Albany, New York, serving over two hundred parishes in a geographically large diocese that spread from the Pennsylvania border and the northern reaches of the

Appalachian Mountains to deep in the Adirondack
in villages and cities like Schoharie and Green Island
Falls and Lake George and Saratoga Springs and Herkimer and
Schenectady—places widely diverse in their populations and expe-
riences of church. Later, I did similar work for the Archdiocese of
San Francisco, an area hardly known for its heterogeneity.

Time after time, in parish after parish, in countless meetings
with parish staffs, pastoral councils, youth ministry leadership
teams, and thousands of different parishioners, the one comment
guaranteed to be made in every case was, "Our parish is unique."
Of course! It is true! Every parish is unique! Even two parishes in
the densest of cities, sitting just down the street from one another,
serving similar demographic populations, will have evolved differently, with different experiences, different leadership, different parishioners. No two ever move in quite the same directions.

Of course, many similarities will also exist. We are, after all,
all humans, we are all Catholics. But each parish needs to set its
own course. Each needs to write its own mission statement, cultivate its own leaders, determine its own programs. You can and
should learn from one another, but you cannot copy one another.
Ownership of change comes only after sweating blood together in
finding the path which works the best for your unique group. You
will know when you have found it. There will be a moment when
each person on the planning team will be able to look around
and realize that collectively, together, you found your way. If you're
really lucky, you'll see tongues of flame from the Holy Spirit or perhaps only glowing light bulbs above each head as the group experiences a collective "Aha!" moment, but there have been very few
such reports lately.

One issue towers over all others in determining the ability to
make sustained change in the parish: the attitude of the pastor. It is
the key to success in nearly every issue discussed in this book. It is,
after all, the pastor's faith that ignites and animates the faith of the

members of the church. By extension, his leadership style and his personality do as well. One convert was overheard to say, "I didn't join *the* Catholic Church. I joined *this* Catholic church." For better or for worse.

This is neither a condemnation of pastors nor of the Catholic Church. It is just as true with Protestant churches as with Catholic ones. Think of well-known megachurches that have suffered great loss of membership or have collapsed completely when the charismatic minister died or was perhaps caught up in scandal. Think of vibrant Catholic parishes that have done the same when a dynamic pastor moved to another location.

No pastor will stay at one parish forever. No pastor is immortal. He will retire, perhaps he will become ill and be replaced, or he will die. Change will happen at some point. Some steps can be taken to prevent all the movement made from being lost.

1. Seek full and complete pastor ownership of every step toward parish renewal. Change cannot be a tolerated side movement, separate from the mainstream life of the parish. There cannot be an upstairs church and a downstairs church. Pastor ownership will assure that he communicates your hopes to the bishop as he prepares to appoint a replacement.

2. Seek broad, consensual ownership for parish decision making so that the new pastor hears the dreams of the laity from the beginning of his term.

3. If the parish has more than one priest, or if the parish has a deacon, make certain that they are integrally involved in decision making and a broad array of ministries. After all, they will stay when the pastor departs.

4. Make certain that large numbers of parishioners are involved in ministry leadership at all levels so that all ministries are sustained without the leadership of the departed pastor.

5. Make certain that the structures for identifying, inviting, forming and training, and supporting lay ministers are firmly in place; nurturing structures, above all. Lay ministers must never find themselves alone. The parish must always care for them to keep them refreshed and renewed.

6. Invite constant prayer from parishioners for an outcome in selecting a new pastor that meets the needs of all.

7. Whenever the occasion arises, try to develop a personal relationship with your bishop. When he is present in your parish for confirmation, reach out to him. Talk with him. Listen to him. Let him come to know what makes your parish unique. Perhaps when he needs to make the decision about a new pastor for your parish, he will remember his encounter with you.

8. When a change in pastorate inevitably comes, make certain that diocesan officials hear the voices of all parishioners through authentic listening sessions filled with articulate parishioners who have been prepared for the meetings. Written documentation should be prepared and given to the diocesan Personnel Board and should do the following:
    *   Describes the structures for faith development of parishioners and ministers,
    *   Stresses the need to keep these processes in place, and
    *   Seeks certain qualities in the new pastor that will help this happen.

Of course, none of these steps will guarantee that a new pastor will continue the movement made by the former one. Inevitably, he will take some different direction. He has a right to do so. He will on occasion thrill some parishioners and at other times disappoint or even infuriate them with his new positions. After all, as much as shared decision-making methods may be used, the church is not a democracy. The pastor is still the ultimate decision maker.

In the final analysis, each Catholic must make a personal, conscientious decision about the particular parish in which he or she will seek to live out an authentic Catholic life. This is the moment when each person must become a servant leader and try to make this decision as free from reasons of pride or disappointment or anger as possible. Changing parishes should be the last resort and should be based upon a conviction that it is no longer possible to share one's gifts at the old parish. Leaving can be done with love and thanks and honor. One can say "Goodbye," close one chapter in life's book, take along a rich treasure of experiences, and open a new chapter in a new parish.

Having considered that possibility, you now begin the process of making your parish a great one. Go back to the Foreword of this book. Reread the eighteen steps toward change. Immerse yourself in the many stories, plans, recommendations, and admonitions in these twenty-two chapters. Think again about how to begin. How will you spread the word that you want to meet with and listen to people? How will you get the pastor on board? How will you determine a planning team?

To paraphrase what the great American writer Thomas Wolfe said (eliminating some of the sexist language of his era), "What Christ is saying always, what he never swerves from saying, what he says a thousand times and in a thousand different ways, but always with a central unity of belief, is this: I am my Father's son and you are my brothers and sisters. And the unity that binds us all together, that makes this earth a family, and all of us brothers and sisters, and so, the children of God, is love."

Isn't that what we want of our parish? Remember that image at the beginning of the Foreword of this book: A large circle of believers, a circle that faces both inward and outward, at once joyfully celebrating shared convictions and always inviting others to join the circle. Remember Father Greeley's definition: Love and Life and Friendship and Celebration make Church.

Great parishes have great circles of believers, filled with faith, hope and love, who shout out in celebration. Ordinary parishes don't.

Great parishes are vibrant and exciting and diverse and surprising and fun to belong to. Ordinary parishes aren't.

Great parishes flourish and grow. Ordinary parishes shrivel up and blow away or, at the very least, become irrelevant.

Simplify things. Keep these images in your mind. And, once again, swallow hard, breathe deeply, and begin! May the peace of Christ be with you always.

Good News Parish Leadership: *Trust-Building Guidelines, Tools, and Ideas*
REV. MICHAEL L. PAPESH

Michael Papesh highlights four essential elements of good news pastoral leadership: ongoing pastoral planning, discernment decision-making, broad and gracious hospitality, and trust building. A fascinating and challenging book for pastoral leaders, associates, pastoral council members, and all who are involved in and committed to parish life.

280 pages ■ $19.95 ■ order 957057 ■ 9781585957057

Dreams and Visions: *Pastoral Planning for Lifelong Faith Formation*
BILL HUEBSCH

Here Bill urges parish leaders and ministers to move in the direction of lifelong faith formation by offering parishioners powerful conversion experiences. He also offers a clear and consistent plan for step-by-step growth, with special emphasis on excellent liturgies, strong and effective catechist and teacher formation, and developing households of faith.

144 pages ■ $14.95 ■ order 956388 ■ 9781585956388

When They Come Home: *Ways to Welcome Returning Catholics*
MELANIE RIGNEY and ANNA M. LANAVE

Here the authors offer practical, how-to advice on building parish programs that will attract inactive Catholics and keep them engaged once they've returned. Returnees, they say, will be richer for rekindling their relationship with Christ and the parish will be richer for sharing their journey.

96 pages ■ $9.95 ■ order 957613 ■ 9781585957613

Welcome the People: *Ways to Gather and Nourish Adult Catholics*
JIM SMITH

Feeding the fire of adult faith demands from parish leaders a burning desire in their own hearts, as well as imagination and courage. Far more than a dry manual, this book offers an uncomplicated process for action and renewed faith as well as an abundance of ways to gather and nourish adult Catholics.

128 pages ■ $12.95 ■ order 957071 ■ 9781585957071

TWENTY THIRD 23rd

1-800-321-0411 ■ WWW.23RDPUBLICATIONS.COM